YOUR SECOND DRAFT

How to Be Your Own Editor

ALEX KOURVO

LOVELY DAY
BOOKS

Your Second Draft: How to Be Your Own Editor

Lovely Day Books

© 2025 Alex Kourvo

AlexKourvo.com

Excerpt from *Tempting Taste* by Sara Whitney. © 2020 by Sara Whitney. Published by LoveSpark Press. Reprinted with permission from the author.

ISBN: 9781956107159 (paperback)

Contents

Your Second Draft

How to Be Your Own Editor

ONE

Where to Start

Anyone who finishes writing a novel—of any quality—should be proud. The number of people who start novels is enormous. The number who finish a full first draft is tiny. The number of people who go on to revise and polish those drafts is smaller yet.

Joining this elite club takes hard work and dedication. You'll have to learn new skills and cultivate new levels of patience. But it will be so, so worth it.

The hardest part of revising a rough draft is knowing where to start. Too many authors jump directly into copyedits without first addressing the big structural edit their novel needs. These writers begin their revisions by opening chapter one and "perfecting" it before moving on to chapter two. They then "perfect" chapter two before moving on to chapter three—or worse yet, cycle back to chapter one again.

These writers are letting their fear get the better of them. They know, deep down, that their novels have structural issues. However, it's easier to do copyedits. After all, copyedits are straightforward, with rules that everyone agrees on. We all learned spelling and grammar in school. We know how to pass that class.

A good developmental edit is hard. We don't have absolute rules to follow, only guidelines. A hundred authors will never agree on the best way to express theme, or handle a midpoint scene, or reveal character. How do you know if you're doing it right? For many writers, it seems far safer to fiddle with sentences and word choice than to take a hard look at the novel as a whole.

However, when you're revising a novel, you should start by taking a step back to look at the big picture. Have you written a three-dimensional hero with interesting problems? Have you pitted him against a worthy adversary? Are the stakes high? Are the scenes in the right order? Does the book come to an epic climax?

After these bigger issues are taken care of, it's time to turn to medium-sized issues like vivid description and dialogue that crackles on the page. Are your characters consistent? Is the theme appropriate for the genre? Is the writing confident? Do the scenes begin and end well?

The draft that comes between the rough draft and the polish is the hardest draft, but also the most magical. This is where the story comes into focus. You're moving big chunks of prose around, and rethinking your initial assumptions about character and plot. Motivations get stronger. Plots are streamlined. Characters become more realistic. Theme becomes clear. In the second draft, you're no longer spinning out the story, hoping to get from "once upon a time" to "the end." Now is your chance to shape what you have on the page, making it better with each pass. The second draft is where the novel on the page starts to match the vision of the novel in your head. And if that isn't magic, I don't know what is.

You get as many do-overs as you want at this stage. A second draft requires a lot of changing, rearranging, and filling in. Some very experienced authors can do all of that at once, but that's not the norm. Most authors require more than one pass to get it right—especially when changing something in chapter five breaks something in chapter fifteen, and vice-versa. When I say "your second draft" I mean everything that happens between the raw first draft of getting the words down on the page, and the final draft, where you're doing copyedits and proofreading. How long you spend in this middle phase of writing isn't important. Getting the story shaped to your satisfaction is.

I'm Here to Help

I'm passionate about novels. I read them, write them, edit them, review them, and talk about them with my friends. I've been an editor for fifteen years, working for small presses and private clients. In addition, I've taught over a hundred writing workshops. Nothing makes me happier than helping new writers.

The purpose of *Your Second Draft* is to take an objective look at your novel, the way a developmental editor would. We're not here to make your novel perfect. There's no such thing as perfect. But we can agree on some best practices to make your book appealing to readers. I want everyone to have the confidence to submit to publishers or self-publish a novel, knowing their book is the best they could make it.

Now the Bad News

There's no substitute for being your own editor.

If you're pursuing traditional publishing, the agents and editors you approach expect a fully edited book to land on their desks. Agents and publishers are drowning in "good enough" novels, or novels with "potential." They don't need more novels that are merely good enough. The less they have to work on a novel, the less time and effort they'll have to spend, and therefore, the more profitable the book will be for them. Because the supply exceeds the demand, they hold out for novels they can sell with minimal effort.

If you're self-publishing, the bar is even higher. Here, you're competing head-to-head with traditionally published books, but you won't have any of the resources of a publishing company, such as editors, cover designers, and publicists. You'll need to hire your own editor if you indie publish.

Editors are absolutely worth the cost, but professional editing is expensive. It takes an editor a lot of time and a lot of expertise to edit a novel, and the price reflects that. Ironically, an editor is most useful to a writer who's already done most of the work. An editor busy correcting basic flaws can't put her energy into honing your work. Therefore, it's crucial that an author doesn't try to hire an editor too early in the process. Editors *are* worth your time and money, but only after you've done the heavy lifting yourself.

The problem is, authors aren't taught how to edit their own work, especially when it comes to big-picture stuff like plot structure and character arc. School teaches you to analyze literature on the sentence and paragraph level, rather than looking at the story as a whole.

When writers begin working on novels, many of them join critique groups, which is awesome, but critique groups will only read a few pages at a time, perhaps ten pages a week at most. Critique groups are great at zeroing in on small problems within a chapter, but your critique partners never see the way the chapters fit together.

Even beta readers, who read the entire novel at once, sometimes can't see the forest for the trees. They're good at pointing out problems, but less good at explaining *why* something isn't working, and they almost never come up with workable solutions, because it isn't their book.

The second draft is all on you, but editing a complete novel can be a lonely business. Don't expect any public cheerleading for your editing process. While you're drafting, you can go on social media and say, "I wrote 1250 words today!" or "I wrote 500 words in my last writing sprint!" Your friends will fall over themselves to like your post and give you kudos. However, if you tell your friends, "I clarified my antagonist's motivation," or, "I made my story stakes stronger," you'll get crickets. Your friends still like you and they still support your efforts, but nobody knows how to quantify editing. Drafting is measurable. You either have words on the page or you don't. Editing is fuzzy. Sometimes, your best editing days are when you *lose* word count.

Your novel is going to get better with each pass, and better yet after your beta readers and your editor weigh in, but the revision is up to you, and you alone.

The Revision Mindset

You write your rough draft with your gut. You copy-edit with your brain. But you revise your second draft with your *heart*. You're going to have to bring your whole self to this part of the process, including sincere emotion. You can't revise with a cynical mindset. You're uncovering the true essence of your story, and that can't be faked.

It's normal to feel a bit overwhelmed at this stage. The best way to handle it is to plan your revision and give yourself plenty of time. It always takes longer to complete a second draft than you assume it will.

Revision takes focus. It's nearly impossible to revise a novel in fits and starts. You need to block out big chunks of time when you can immerse yourself in the story. This is a very different skill set from drafting. You're going to have to use all of your discipline, creativity, and confidence to finish your second draft. Give your book every chance of success by scheduling the time you need to do it justice.

There will be days you feel like you're moving backwards. Revising is a messy process, with lots of stops and starts. Sometimes you have to cut passages you love if they no longer serve the story. Sometimes you'll find plot holes that require many chapters to fill.

Looking at the big picture means facing every single problem in your novel all at once. You're going to *fix* the problems one at a time, but you have to *consider* them all at once. By its very nature, editing is a critical exercise. You're purposely telling yourself everything that's wrong with your work. Don't let yourself get bogged down in negativity. Writing a complete novel is hard. Revising that novel is even harder. And publishing is a minefield of rejection and doubt.

Whatever you do, don't go into a downward spiral.

Even if you're having a bad day. Even if you cut a chapter you loved. Even if you rewrote an entire page, only to realize it worked better in the original. Don't let your brain associate your novel with negativity. That's a one-way path to procrastination and writer's block.

Don't ever call your novel "bad" or say that it's "crap." No, it is *not*. Is it flawed? Yes. Is it fixable? Also yes. You're putting in the work of a second draft because you believe in your novel and you believe in its potential. I believe in it too.

A Note About the Examples

My examples come from popular and classic fiction. I've relied on bestsellers, award-winning novels, and novels that have become movies. Popularity isn't always a mark of quality, but there was something in these books that made millions of readers want to read them, making them ideal examples. I credit the authors, because I'm talking about the *books*, not the movies that were made from them.

There will be spoilers.

When I discuss storytelling patterns, I'm only qualified to speak about novels that were written in English for a Western audience. There are other storytelling patterns in other parts of the world that are beyond the scope of this book.

The words *hero, heroine,* and *protagonist* are used

interchangeably in this book, because heroism has no gender, and anyone can save the world.

About the Exercises

Each chapter ends with exercises to help you take a second look at your manuscript. You can do them in any order, since revision isn't a linear process. You may need to repeat steps if your revision takes your story in a new direction.

Most of the exercises can be done directly on your manuscript, using whatever notation or margin comments your software provides. A few will require a separate document or notebook.

Many of the exercises will ask you to check things to make sure you've done them. We're all guilty of thinking our stories are complete simply because they're complete in our imagination. What we imagine isn't always on the page. When the exercise says, "point to the page where…" I mean you should actually put your finger on the page or highlight the exact passage on your computer. Can't find the passage on the page? This is your opportunity to mark where things *should* be when your revision is complete.

First Steps

When embarking on a second draft, make a copy of your first draft and put it in a separate folder. It's easier to revise with abandon when you know you can go back to the original if you need to. You won't, by the way—go back to it, I mean. But knowing that you *can* go back to your rough draft gives you the courage to make big, bold changes.

Next, make an outline. Not an outline of what you think is in the manuscript, but an outline of what you actually wrote. It shouldn't be long or detailed. Two or three sentences per scene is plenty. You could write something like, "Eugene is given his final warning at work. He tells his boss to go to hell and gets fired on the spot. Later, Dominic finds him drunk at the Buttonhole Pub, and drives him home."

Even if you're a plotter who outlined the novel before you began, I guarantee that the story has changed along the way. You need a broad overview of your novel as it exists right now, and this is the easiest way to get it.

Finally, you'll write your own editorial letter, just as if you were your own editor. An editorial letter is a list of all the issues that your book has. It's your plan for revision.

Just as your outline is for your eyes only, so is this letter. Write it any way you want. Checklist? Bullet points? Lots of details? Do whatever works best for you. The purpose of this document is to take the anxiety out of editing by breaking it down into achievable goals.

Your list will be long, but you don't have to tackle it

all at once. Do one thing on your list, cross it off, feel a sense of achievement, and then go on to the next. The most important thing about starting your revision is that you have to *start it*. Somewhere. Anywhere. Pick up your pen, or put your fingers on your keyboard, take a deep breath, and begin.

A Second Look

1. Commit to the process of revision. Understand that the process is messy and time-consuming, and lean into that. See it as an opportunity, not a chore. Promise yourself that you'll play with possibilities rather than remain tethered to the manuscript as it exists right now.

2. Make a copy of your manuscript. Call it version 1.0 and save it in a separate folder. Remind yourself that you get as many do-overs as you want, and nothing will destroy what you've already created.

3. Put revision sessions on your calendar. It's hard to edit your novel in fits and starts, so plan for large blocks of time if you can. Gather support from your writing community. Tell your friends what kind of cheerleading you need, so they can support you.

4. Make a scaled-down outline of your novel as it exists right now. List each scene and write two or three sentences about what happens, including action, thought, and emotion. This can be a spreadsheet, bullet points, or any other format that works for you.

TWO

The Protagonist

The better you know your protagonist, the better your book will be. When you know your heroine deeply, you know her strengths and flaws. You know what will stress her out, cause her the most trouble, and make her face her deepest fears. You know how she can change and grow to become her best self. In other words, great characters make great plots.

The better you know your heroine, the more realistically you can portray her on the page. And the more realistically you portray her on the page, the more readers will like your book. When revising, your goal is to make a three-dimensional heroine whose actions and motivations make sense. Readers want to go on a story journey with a character they like, trust, and root for.

Making a Protagonist Three-Dimensional

Readers won't finish a book if they don't like the heroine, or at least relate to her on some level. It's not enough for you to love your heroine. You need to help the reader love her too.

You can make her kind, or clever, or helpful, but those are vague traits. Most of the people we know are kind, and clever, and helpful. What makes your protagonist stand out in a crowd? What are her strong beliefs and unshakable values? What does she care about more than anything in the world? What can she do better than anyone else? Be specific. Don't focus on who she *is*. Instead, show us what she *does*.

Don't tell the reader that your heroine is dependable. Show her picking up her brother at the airport even though the flight was three hours late and her brother forgot to text when he landed. Don't tell us that your heroine is a good listener. Show her patiently sitting through her aunt's fifth repetition of her latest medical scare, and then gently steering the conversation toward less upsetting topics. When you're revising, you should be able to point to the exact page that shows your heroine's positive qualities.

In *The Devil Wears Prada* by Lauren Weisberger, the heroine, Andrea, is fresh out of college, eager to make it in New York. She's loyal, hardworking, and smart. The reader sees it—not because the author told us so, but because she showed us in what Andrea says, what she does, and what she thinks. We see her loyalty, as she keeps the same friends she had in college. We see her ambition as she puts in fourteen-hour days at her job. We see how smart she is in her witty commentary on everything going on at *Runway* magazine.

Lessons in Chemistry by Bonnie Garmus is about a scientist named Elizabeth Zott who lives in California in the 1950s. She's brilliant, and always speaks her mind, both to her peers and to her employers. She's straightforward and honest, and doesn't care what anyone else thinks of her, even if it means she eats lunch alone every day. She makes her own way in the male-dominated work world, holding her own against the sexist men around her. When her bosses neglect to give her the equipment they promised her, she takes cases of beakers from a better-equipped lab in the building, daring them to object. Her willingness to ignore social norms means she can successfully raise her daughter as a single mom at a time when this was considered shameful.

If readers like and believe in the heroine, they'll keep reading, even if the plot is lacking. Readers will remember stellar characters long after they've forgotten the particulars of the plot. Show your heroine's most attractive and relatable qualities right up front.

But whatever you do, don't make your protagonist perfect. Readers want to watch your protagonist grow and change. Heroines need past trauma to overcome, bad habits to break, and fears to fight through.

The problem with many first-draft heroines is that they have flaws that don't fit. Her flaws are randomly thrown in to make her look "well-rounded." So suddenly your heroine can't dance, or she's afraid of heights, or she's short-tempered, or a bad driver. This isn't going to make your heroine seem three-dimensional. It's going to make her seem scattered.

Instead, you should look at the heroine's strengths and turn them upside down. That's where you'll find the perfect flaw to give her. The only flaws that matter are the ones that go hand-in-hand with her strengths.

Does your heroine see the best in everyone? That also means she's naïve, and easily exploited. Is she hardworking and ambitious? Watch for the ways her personal life and relationships suffer for it. Is she good at keeping peace between people? Don't count on her to stand up to injustice, even when she really should.

In *The Devil Wears Prada*, we see that Andrea's strengths match her flaws one-to-one. She's hardworking and eager to prove herself, which also means she neglects her friends, neglects her boyfriend, and loses herself in the process. She's smart, but she's booksmart. She isn't self-aware enough to see how she's being exploited. She's loyal, which is great, except she finds herself loyal to a very bad boss.

Elizabeth Zott from *Lessons in Chemistry* is straightforward and honest. She doesn't care about other people's opinions, which makes her terrible at reading social cues. She blurts out inappropriate remarks, gets in trouble at work, and can't make friends. She doesn't understand how dangerous certain men in her life are, and comes close to getting assaulted on two occasions. Although she's a good mom, she doesn't know how to guide her daughter through the social life of school.

You can give your heroine any strengths. You can give her any flaws. But one is always the mirror of the other. When you're revising, look at your hero or heroine's personality and make sure that every flaw has an upside, and every strength has a cost. More than anything else, this will make your characters believable. When books, classes, and teachers say you need to make your protagonist three-dimensional, this strength/flaw duality is what they're talking about.

Introducing a Protagonist

Your hero is complex, of course, with many facets to his personality, but chapter one is where you shine a spotlight on the strongest part. What's his number one defining characteristic? Is he ambitious? Is he organized? Protective? Sophisticated? Creative?

Check your first chapter. Have you shown the reader what kind of person your hero is? He'll grow and change throughout the book, but his deep-down core doesn't change, and the reader needs to see a glimpse of that right away.

In *The Martian* by Andy Weir, astronaut Mark Watney has several qualities that make him a great hero. He's smart, especially in science and engineering. He's funny. He's self-aware. But his number-one defining characteristic is that he's determined.

We see that determination in chapter one, page one. When the book opens, Watney is not only stranded alone, but he's out in a sandstorm, he's badly injured, and his spacesuit is failing. He should be dead, but by the end of chapter one, he's patched his suit, he's made it into the habitat, and he's given himself nine stitches. He's already thinking about communication with Earth. He's not just determined to survive, he's determined to get off Mars.

Notice that all this comes in the form of an active scene. *The Martian* doesn't start with description, or explanation, or backstory. It's a scene. It's very in-the-moment, using all five senses, dialogue, character movement, and the hero's thoughts and feelings. That's the best way to introduce a hero. You can explain his backstory later.

Take another look at your opening scene. Make sure you've introduced your hero using an active scene, that you're playing up his strengths, and that you've shown him doing something very "on brand" for the character.

Getting to Know Your Protagonist

By the end of act one—about 20-25% of the way through your book—readers should feel like they know your hero. They know what his life circumstances are, and why he needs to change them. They know his attitudes, his values, and his quirks. They know what he wants and how far he's willing to go to get it.

Check that you've included scenes of your hero at work (or school), at home, and at play. What does your hero do for a living? Why has he chosen that job? What does he like or dislike about it? Who does he live with? What are the conflicts around that living situation? Play includes hobbies and social gatherings. Your hero can be buying new yarn for a knitting project, or at the bar having drinks with friends.

By the time readers have finished the first quarter of *The Martian*, they've seen Watney in all three settings. Surviving alone on Mars is his daily work. He has to figure out water, food, and shelter, and then turn his attention to communicating with NASA. But readers have also seen his home, as Watney reconfigures his habitat to grow potatoes. In his downtime, he opens the lockers left behind by his crewmates and raids their stashes of entertainment. He's amused by his captain's collection of 1970s TV shows, but soon gets attached to the storylines.

The best and quickest way to get your readers to bond with your hero is by including a "Save the Cat" moment. This is a phrase coined by Blake Snyder that has spread through the writing community. A Save the Cat moment is a scene, early in the book, where the hero does something kind for someone else. The hero isn't acting this way because of a reward, or glory, or profit. He's simply the kind of person who does nice things. It's not part of the main plot. This is a pure character beat.

Part of Your World by Abby Jimenez is about a doctor named Alexis who falls in love with a wood-carver named Daniel. Daniel shows himself to be lovable right from the moment they meet. He volunteers to pull Alexis' car out of a ditch, turning down the forty dollars she tries to pay him for it. Shortly after, Daniel checks on an elderly neighbor who usually shows up at the local diner every morning, but is missing today. The neighbor has had a fall, and Daniel patches him up, tidies his house, and promises to return later to install a grab bar in the shower.

Fourth Wing by Rebecca Yarros is a fantasy novel where teenagers attend a war college to learn how to fly dragons into battle. In order to get into the school, the students have to cross a dangerous, slippery foot-bridge over a deep canyon. It's the first test, and many of them don't pass. As the students are standing in line to cross, the heroine, Violet, notices that the girl next to her is wearing boots with smooth soles. She will certainly slip off the narrow bridge when she attempts her crossing. Violet trades her left boot for the other girl's boot, so they each have one good boot and one bad one. This makes Violet's own crossing more dangerous, but saves the other girl.

A Save the Cat moment can be anything. It can be waking up early on Saturday to volunteer in a soup kitchen. It can be a New Yorker helping a tourist find her subway stop. It can be inviting a lonely neighbor over for dinner, even though the heroine knows her neighbor will complain about traffic regulations for three hours. Whatever it is, it should fit the theme and tone of the book, so the reader effortlessly falls in love with your hero.

A Protagonist Must Be Active

Good fiction places a hero into a brand-new situation, with problems that will test him to his limits. The beginning of a novel often shows obstacles thrown at the hero faster than he can cope with them. That's fine in the short term. However, no reader wants to read about a sad sack who has misery heaped upon him. Readers want to read about characters who rise to the occasion, form a plan, and deal with these new problems head-on. The sooner you put your hero into action, the better.

Even if he's reacting to unfolding events, your protagonist should still be actively pursuing his goal. A hero needs to make decisions. A hero needs to try. In short, a hero needs agency. Without the hero's agency, you don't have a story. All you've got is a list of events.

Agency essentially means your protagonist is in charge of the direction the plot moves in. This might sound obvious, but authors often outline a great story, and then move the hero through it like they're playing a video game. A hero needs to want something. Desperately. And he has to be willing to upend his life to get it. This should be true for the big turning point scenes as well as in smaller moments.

Little Brother by Cory Doctorow is about a teenage computer hacker named Marcus. In chapter three, he's on the subway with his friends when a bomb goes off. Everyone is running and panicking, but it's Marcus who takes action and steers his friends to safety, away from the bomb shelters and toward the stairs leading to the surface. While his friends are asking, "What should we do?" Marcus is the one with a plan. The bomb going off is something that happens *to* the hero. But Marcus immediately starts working to get himself and his friends out of the subway. He's the proactive character.

There are slower scenes where your characters need to regroup and plan, especially in the aftermath of a big turning point in the story. Characters need time to process their emotions and gather strength. But even in these regrouping scenes, the hero should be the one making the decision to move forward, and should have a plan for doing so.

One way to check if your hero is active enough is to count how many mistakes he makes. You've got a flawed hero trying to solve a problem he's never faced before, so he's going to get it wrong at first. Making things worse is what heroes do best. Those mistakes teach him exactly what he needs to learn. Make sure your hero is the one steering the ship, even if he's steering it into a hurricane.

Show Change on the Page

A protagonist's choices and actions should change them. The person they are at the beginning of the story isn't able to achieve their goal. They have to learn and grow through the story journey. Only then are they capable of success. Your plot forces that character change.

Show the character's growth, don't just tell the reader about it. It needs to be shown in action, not thought. Phrases like "she suddenly realized..." or "he thought long and hard until..." are not good enough. Your hero should *do* something that contrasts with the person he was before, especially if it's something he's always wanted to do, but felt unworthy of.

Maybe your protagonist finally manages to ask their crush out on a date. Or says "no" when their boss asks them to work late for the third time this week. Maybe they move to another country. Or they finally get that pet pig they've always wanted. Readers love it when they see a protagonist do something at the end of the book that they weren't capable of in chapter one.

Legends and Lattes by Travis Baldree is a cozy fantasy about an orc named Viv who gives up being a sword-for-hire to open a coffee shop. In order to get started, she kills a giant spider and takes a precious stone from it, because it's meant to bestow luck. Viv is a loner who doesn't trust anyone, not even her crew-mates in the raid. She picks up the stone and leaves them behind without a word. She buries the lucky stone under the floor of her new coffee shop, and she constantly frets about her secret getting out.

By the end of the novel, Viv is different. She's built a thriving coffee shop, and has a found family whom she trusts completely. She's made amends with her old crew. She comes clean about her lucky stone, and real-izes that she doesn't need it anymore, because the community around her is all the luck she needs. Letting go of the stone is a powerful symbol of her growth.

If you're looking for a subtle way to show, rather than tell character change, you can show how the minor characters react to the heroine's new behavior. It's very rare in life that people muster up the courage to make a big change, so the other characters will certainly notice. Her best friend might congratulate your heroine on her new exercise habit after a lifetime of laziness. A co-worker might give her kudos for standing up to their terrible boss. A sibling might comment on the confidence and sparkle the heroine exhibits.

As you're revising, mark the passages that contrast the old and the new. Your readers need to see exactly how your heroine has changed. Find an action or behavior in act one and show its opposite in the resolution. Readers will love the sense that this story journey has been worthwhile, and that the heroine has become her best self.

Multiple Protagonists

Some stories are so complex that one hero simply isn't enough to showcase the full experience. It can be tempting to tell your story from multiple points of view, and even elevate those other viewpoints to true hero status. But think long and hard before using multiple heroes, because it always seems easier than it is.

You'll have to do more character development and research. You'll have to make sure that each point of view feels necessary and unique. Each protagonist must have his own story arc, where the events of the story force him to change and grow.

You'll need room to do this. It takes more pages to write about more heroes, and a book can become too long for the marketplace. Multiple protagonists are more common in fantasy, science fiction, historical fiction, and big family sagas. These books often come in series, where the author has many books to develop many character arcs.

An important exception is the contemporary romance, where it's common to have chapters alternate point of view between the two lovers. However, in the case of romance, the two lovers are telling one story, with their character arcs moving in tandem. The plots are streamlined, with a narrow focus on the unfolding relationship, so these books are short.

When revising a story that has multiple points of view, make sure that each character is distinct on the page. A reader should be able to tell whose head they're in by the way the character thinks, by what she does, and by what she says. Give your characters strong, unique opinions, and let them voice those opinions in dialogue and thought. Readers should never have to guess whose point of view they're in, or flip back pages to reorient themselves.

Each point of view character needs to offer new information—something the other point of view characters don't know. But this new viewpoint shouldn't exist simply to feed new information to the reader. These characters also need their own motivations, their own desires, and their own struggles. Each character must have a unique perspective on the plot conflict.

How many points of view does a novel need? How many heroes? When it comes to characters, you want to use as few as possible. Ask yourself if your story *must* be told with several protagonists. Remember that a new point of view character is not necessarily a new *hero*. You can have chapters from a secondary character's point of view, but still have one main hero. The hero is the person who has the most to lose, and the person who solves the story problem.

An example of a story with multiple protagonists is *Station Eleven* by Emily St. John Mandel. *Station Eleven* takes place twenty years after a deadly plague has killed ninety percent of humans. While society tries to rebuild itself, Kirsten Raymonde travels from settlement to settlement with a group of actors, performing shows for people who need culture and enrichment in a tough time.

Station Eleven is also about an actor named Arthur, who was patient zero for the plague. His life and Kirsten's life intersect in interesting ways, even after his death. Kirsten is the protagonist, but so is Arthur. They each have a complete story arc. There are also chapters from the points of view of some of the minor characters. Each one brings new information to the story, and each has a new perspective about what's really going on, but they aren't elevated to true protagonist status. The author included their perspective to enrich and complete the story, but these minor characters don't change. Arthur and Kirsten do.

The Martian also has multiple points of view, but only one protagonist. The majority of the book is from Watney's point of view. Three-quarters of the chapters are his. His story is interspersed with chapters that take place on Earth, from the point of view of the employees of NASA, who are trying to bring him home. They have information and perspective that

Watney doesn't have. But this is Mark Watney's story. He's the hero. He's the one with the story arc, and he's the one who solves the story problem.

When you're revising a novel with multiple protagonists, write down their separate character arcs. Do they grow in unique ways? Do they both solve the story problem, or could one of them solve it without the other?

It's difficult to write multiple points of view, and even more difficult to write multiple *heroes*. If you've written a draft with multiple protagonists, think about combining a few of them. Don't make more work for yourself unless it's absolutely necessary.

Exceptional Protagonists

Sometimes, protagonists aren't heroic in the conventional sense. Sometimes our stories call for protagonists who don't have worthy goals, or don't have a moral compass, or don't change much from book to book. These stories feature antiheroes or their good guy counterparts, eternal heroes. You'll often see antiheroes in literary fiction, grimdark fantasy, and noir mystery, while eternal heroes are common in cozy mystery and thriller series.

Antiheroes have grown in popularity over the years, not only in novels, but in movies and TV too. Living among other humans is hard, and morality is complicated. Readers are hungry for stories that tackle these issues. But writing an antihero isn't simply a matter of flipping the script and telling the story from the bad guy's point of view. It's trickier than that, and writing an antihero is more difficult than writing a traditional hero or heroine.

Don't forget the "hero" part of antihero. Help your readers identify with your antihero by emphasizing his best qualities. It helps if he's funny. Antiheroes are often great observers of human nature, and love to point out hypocrisy. They often say things that the rest of us wish we could say out loud.

Lawrence Block has written a series about a hitman named Keller. Keller kills people—not because he's compelled to, or to right a wrong, but because he's paid to do it. Readers love Keller because he's self-aware, funny, kind, and extremely wise about human nature. Ironically, he's learned how to be fully human, even though he ends other humans' lives.

An antihero doesn't care about idealism or conventional morality. He will give in to his selfish desires of the moment rather than thinking about the long-term good. It's not that he's evil. He's pragmatic, believing the ends justify the means. But unlike a true villain, an antihero has lines he won't cross. He has a personal code he lives by. For example, Keller won't kill children or pets, even if he's hired to. It's a *very* low bar. When your protagonist is an antihero, you can make the bar as low as you want, as long as there is one.

Although the antihero doesn't care what society

says is right or wrong, be sure you've given your anti-hero *something* to care about. Whether it's a sibling, a lover, a hometown, or a pet, the antihero is all about protecting what he loves the most. In the first book in the *Hitman* series, Keller gets a dog. The stakes are raised even higher later in the series when Keller gets married and has a daughter. Can he keep being a killer-for-hire when he has a family?

It's not easy to write a great antihero, but it helps if you can make him as relatable as possible, to give readers a bad guy they can't help but root for. When you're revising, pick out places that show the antihero doing something likable, relatable, or funny. Draw out those sections as much as you can.

The flip side of an antihero is an eternal hero. These are the heroes who are so much larger than life that they represent universal values. Think of Sherlock Holmes, who represents intelligence, or Atticus Finch, who represents integrity, or Phryne Fisher, who represents feminism. These characters are human, and three-dimensional, but they're very different from a traditional hero.

Most novels are about character growth, showing how a character has become a better person through the story journey. But when you have an eternal hero, you don't need that kind of character development. An eternal hero is already in her final form when the story begins.

You'll most often find eternal heroes in plot-heavy

genres like mystery and thriller. Readers of these genres don't *want* their heroes to change. They want their heroes to stay basically the same from book to book through a series.

Eternal heroes are already strong and capable when the story begins, and they're often called in because they're the only ones able to handle the current story problem. They're confident they can pull this off because it's not their first rodeo. They've been solving these kinds of problems for years, and they're awesome at it. Jack Reacher doesn't have to learn how to be a badass. He comes to the page with his skill set already in place. Sherlock Holmes is already the greatest detective of Victorian London. James Bond is already the world's best spy.

If your protagonist is an eternal hero, make sure he's not merely an observer. He must be the catalyst for the change the world needs. Something always has to change in fiction. Change leads to tension and tension is what makes the readers turn the page. The eternal hero doesn't change, but the world changes because of his actions.

The most common place to see an eternal hero or heroine is in a long-running series, but pay attention to how those series start. Often, in the first book, the heroine goes through a traditional character arc. She changes. She grows. This is her origin story. You can see this in book one of the Phryne Fisher series by Kerry Greenwood and the Percy Jackson series by Rick

Riordan. However, in later books, the heroine has transformed into an eternal heroine. She's already had her growth in book one. She's already learned her lessons. She's already leveled up.

From book two onward, she's ready to change the world.

The Right Protagonist for Your Story

When you're revising your novel, you can't separate your hero from the story he's in. A hero's problems must stem directly from who he is, and the plot must be a problem that he is uniquely qualified to solve. A hero should have the traits and flaws he needs to both solve the story problem and to grow by doing so.

An excellent example of this done well is Robert Langdon from *The DaVinci Code* by Dan Brown. The plot of *The DaVinci Code* has Langdon solving a series of tricky puzzles about history, mythology, and religion. He's the perfect person for that role, since he has a PhD in symbology, and is an expert in everything he needs to achieve victory in the world's hardest scavenger hunt. At the same time, he has cut himself off from his spiritual side, becoming pure intellect. The plot of the book helps him connect with the divine feminine and become whole.

The Dashwood sisters from *Sense and Sensibility* by Jane Austen are the perfect heroines for their stories. In Regency England, society is everything, and even those on the edges of it need it badly. The Dashwoods are gentry but poor, meaning a good marriage is the key to stability. Marianne is a dreamy romantic, who's determined to only marry for love. She falls for a charming scoundrel, but she matures through the novel, ultimately marrying a more stable, loving man. Her older sister Elinor is more practical, but even she is foiled by the societal norms of her time, as she thinks she's made a love match with a man who—because of family obligations—is secretly engaged to someone else. In *Sense and Sensibility*, character plus setting equals a plot that keeps readers guessing until the end of the book.

Go back to the short outline you made for your novel at the beginning of your revision process. Read through it again, looking at the way your plot forces your character to grow. If your plot and character aren't working hand-in-hand, think about revising one or the other to bring them more in line. Make sure your hero or heroine is suitable for the story you're putting them in, and make sure you write stories worthy of the amazing characters you've built.

A Second Look

1. List your protagonist's strengths, and the downside of each of those strengths.

2. List your protagonist's flaws, and the advantage that comes with each of those flaws.

3. Examine the lists you made for your protagonist. Do her strengths and flaws match? If not, make a list of ways to make your heroine three-dimensional by making her strengths and flaws mirror each other.

4. Point to the sentences where you've shown both your heroine's strengths and her flaws. If it's not on the page, brainstorm ways you'll show your heroine's strengths and flaws, and mark the places in your manuscript where you'll add them.

5. Write down the big goal that your heroine is trying to reach. Write down all the ways your heroine is uniquely qualified to solve this problem. Mark the places in your manuscript where you've shown this ability. If it's not on the page, brainstorm ways to show it, and mark the place in the manuscript where you'll add it.

6. Open your manuscript to the introduction of your heroine, and make sure her first scene showcases her defining characteristic. If it's not on the page, brainstorm ways to introduce your heroine doing something very on-brand for her. Make that your opening scene.

7. Look through act one and mark the places you've shown your heroine at home, at work, and at play. If those scenes aren't on the page, brainstorm new scenes and mark the places you'll include them.

8. Find your heroine's "Save the Cat" moment. Write down the ways that this moment shows the reader who the heroine is. If there is no Save the Cat moment on the page, brainstorm one for your heroine and mark the place you'll include it in the manuscript.

9. List three ways your hero is different at the end of the story. Point to the pages that contrast the before and after. If you haven't shown that transformation, brainstorm ways to show character change and mark where it will go in the manuscript. If you're writing an eternal hero, show the ways the world around him has changed because of his involvement.

THREE

The Antagonist

Some authors start their books having no idea what the antagonist wants. They start with a hero, and they think up interesting situations and fun one-liners for him, but never give him a worthy adversary. With nobody pushing the hero to act, he doesn't have much to do, and the story stalls out halfway through. What these books need is a well-developed antagonist, with desires as strong as the hero's.

It's hard to put yourself into a villain's shoes. You aren't a bad person, so how should you know what bad people think and do? But fictional antagonists don't think of themselves as bad people either. An antagonist wants something. He wants it just as intensely as the hero wants his goal and will fight just as hard to get it. Villains always think of themselves as heroes who are doing the right thing.

If your antagonist's only desire is to stop the hero,

or thwart the hero, or make the hero miserable, you've got some rewriting to do. A villain always has reasons for what she's doing, and in her mind, those reasons are noble and just. In *The Wizard of Oz*, the Wicked Witch feels entitled to the ruby slippers that belonged to her sister. Why should a stranger who blew in on a tornado have them? The Witch just wants her rightful inheritance and isn't going to let a stranger rob her.

The Purpose of an Antagonist

Heroes don't want to disrupt the world. They want to restore it. In *The Lord of the Rings* by J.R.R. Tolkien, Frodo Baggins never wanted to come into possession of the one ring. Now that he has it, he wants to destroy it to restore peace to the land—and especially to his little village called the Shire. Katniss Everdeen didn't want to join the deadly hunger games. But now that she's in it, she's going to take down the entire system to restore equity to Panem. The four daughters in *The Joy Luck Club* by Amy Tan don't want a life of constant strife with their mothers. They want to understand their mothers, and for their mothers to understand them. They want to restore peace in the family.

Who wants to disrupt the world? Villains. Bad guys. Antagonists. If an antagonist wasn't on the scene to shake up your hero's world, then there would be no story. There would simply be a character living their normal life. Nobody wants to read about normal or mundane or comfortable. They want to read about heroics. That's where villains come in.

Every genre has its favorite antagonists, from the evil terrorist, to the misguided family matriarch, to the sewer-dwelling clown. But what they all have in common is the chaos energy that's bringing unwanted or unhealthy change to the world, with a single-minded forward momentum that will require an equally strong hero to stop them.

The stronger your antagonist is, the better your story will be. Writers love to write great heroes, but without great villains, the heroes would spend the whole story parked in one place. When you're revising, look for ways to make your antagonist bigger, stronger, and even badder. Because when it comes to fiction, antagonists are the fuel that makes your story go.

Qualities of an Antagonist

There are different kinds of antagonists, but they all have three qualities that make them worthy adversaries. They have strong motives, they're more powerful than the hero, and they're ruthless.

No human thinks of herself as evil. Everyone has reasons for what they do and those reasons are justified in our minds. The antagonist's motivations often only make sense to him, but it's important that the antagonist truly believes he's doing the right thing for the right reasons.

In *The Stranger* by Harlan Coben, a villain named Taylor blackmails people who have shameful secrets. If someone doesn't pay up, Taylor reveals the secret to his target's family and friends, ruining their lives. Taylor likes the money, but he likes revealing secrets even more. He often hopes his blackmail victims won't pay up, so he can get their secrets out in the open. He believes the world is a better place when everyone is honest with everyone else, even if the truth is devastating. He thinks he's doing his part to make a healthier society.

In some genres such as literary fiction, women's fiction, and some YA fiction, the antagonist is motivated by love or friendship. This kind of antagonist will do all the wrong things, but do them out of a sincere desire to help the protagonist. In their minds, the hero is going down the wrong path, and needs their help to get back on track. For example, in *The Devil Wears Prada*, Miranda Priestly is "helping" her new assistant learn the ropes. She thinks she has to be hard on Andrea, giving her impossible tasks that make her cry, in order to toughen her up. She wants to be sure that Andrea has what it takes to make it in the competitive world of fashion magazines.

You should be able to point to the passages that show the antagonist's motivation. Help your reader understand why the villain is doing what she's doing, and why she thinks her actions are perfectly justified.

One side note here. I don't have many hard and

fast rules when it comes to writing, but the one I'm about to tell you is non-negotiable. At the big climactic scene, at the crucial moment, never have your hero look at the villain and say, "You're crazy." That's wrong on so many levels. It's ableist language, it's bad storytelling, and it doesn't work. If your villain is doing what she's doing for no reason at all, or for reasons the hero doesn't understand, then you've got some editing to do. A good villain has reasons for what she's doing, and both the hero and the reader understand that motive. Even if the hero thinks the antagonist's motives are total nonsense, or based on trauma that poisons their worldview, he shouldn't act surprised about that fact at the climax scene.

At the beginning of your novel, the antagonist should be in a more powerful position than the heroine. Sometimes the antagonist is physically stronger. The antagonist might have better weapons, bigger armies, or stronger magic. Sometimes the antagonist is smarter or more experienced, possessing insider knowledge that the heroine doesn't have. Sometimes it's an imbalance in structural power, where a boss, teacher, parent, or law enforcement officer has more power than the heroine does. Sometimes the antagonist has higher social standing because of wealth, as in *Pride and Prejudice* by Jane Austen. Or the antagonist has more popularity among her peers, as in *Dork Diaries* by Rachel Renee Russell, where the antagonist is the most popular girl in school and the heroine is a self-described dork.

This is also true for romance, where the two halves of the couple are the antagonists for each other. The couple is often wildly unbalanced. One of them will be richer, professionally superior, above the other one in class, or have insider knowledge. For example, maybe he's a master winemaker, she's a reporter come to do a story on his winery, and he has to teach her about wine. The other half of the couple usually has a different kind of power in the relationship, and those powers are usually complimentary.

When you're revising, make sure your story begins with the scales wildly unbalanced in the antagonist's favor. *Misery* by Stephen King is about a famous writer named Paul Sheldon who is being held prisoner by a deranged fan named Annie Wilkes. He's badly injured, Annie's cabin is out in the country, and there's no way to call for help. She won't let him go until he writes a happy ending for her favorite fictional heroine. Sheldon is powerless in this situation and it looks like Annie is going to get everything she wants.

But you can't just tell the reader that the villain is more powerful, you have to show them. The early scenes with the villain will be a taste of what's to come in the big showdown at the end. Often, in thrillers, there will be a small moment of unwarranted violence, as the bad guy hurts an innocent person or one of his own henchmen. In literary fiction, the antagonist will often say something extremely hurtful that cuts the heroine to the core. An antagonist who is a rival will win a small victory over the heroine. In act one of *Misery*, Annie Wilkes leaves an injured and bedridden Sheldon alone for twenty-four hours without food or medicine, and when she returns, she makes him burn the only copy of his new novel before she'll give him any pain relievers. She's in charge, and everyone knows it.

This power imbalance is going to be reversed at the end of your novel, when the hero levels up to achieve his goal. Unless your novel has an eternal hero, you must leave room for this growth. Readers love to see a hero achieve an impossible goal by defeating a bad guy who's really, really bad.

The antagonist is defending her own interests—professional, economic, romantic, or political. She's defending them hard enough to make herself ruthless. She won't compromise, and is just fine with collateral damage. The antagonist will do *anything* to win. An antagonist lives by the motto, "You can't make an omelet without breaking a few eggs." She believes her cause is so noble that no amount of collateral damage is too high. An antagonist takes hostages. An antagonist hurts other people. This is true whether it's an archvillain trying to take over the world, or an overbearing father who says he'll only pay for college if the heroine gives up her dream of going to art school and becomes a lawyer instead. Even an antagonist who thinks she's working toward the heroine's own good will do horrible things to get there.

This is what makes the antagonist stronger than the heroine. The heroine has scruples, and must find a way to get what she wants without hurting anyone, which puts the heroine in a weaker position. There are lines she won't cross, and the antagonist knows it.

Just as the heroine has a Save the Cat moment, an antagonist needs a "Drown the Puppy" moment where the readers can see for themselves, right there on the page, how ruthless this person is. If you've written a thriller, science fiction, or fantasy novel, this is usually a scene where the villain commits some kind of unwarranted violence. It's harder when you're writing literary fiction or YA where the villain isn't violent, but it can be done. Maybe a sports rival isn't above doing a little cheating. Maybe a parent says something deliberately hurtful in an effort to teach the heroine a lesson. But whatever it is, it must be shown, not told.

Villains Are Varied

Although all antagonists are motivated, powerful, and ruthless, these qualities are expressed in different ways in different genres. Not all antagonists are bad guys. Some are quite good and many of them have the best of intentions.

Thrillers, mysteries, and certain subgenres of science fiction usually have bad guys who are really,

really bad. However, literary fiction, women's fiction, and coming of age stories often have antagonists who are close to the protagonist, and want to "help" the hero "for his own good." Lots of comedies have rivals, who don't want to hurt the hero, but simply out-compete him. Romance novels have the most unique antagonist of all. This is the lover who gets under the heroine's skin, the one she can't stop thinking about, the one who shakes up the heroine's world and turns it upside down, even as he steals her heart.

When you're revising, you need to be clear about your antagonist and which category he fits in. It will help you know how far the antagonist is willing to go to achieve his goals. It also tells you what kind of ending you're aiming toward. Since the antagonist is the energy of the story, understanding his role will help every aspect of your novel. Let's take a look at five kinds of antagonists: the bad guy, the rival, the button pusher, the romantic partner, and the unpersonified antagonist.

Bad Guy

When people hear the word antagonist or villain, they usually think of a classic bad guy. The most well-known and iconic type of villain is a sociopathic killer like Lloyd Hansen in *The Gray Man* by Mark Greaney, or the immortal white supremacists in *Mexican Gothic* by Silvia Moreno-Garcia, or a serial killer like

Hannibal Lecter in *The Silence of the Lambs* by Thomas Harris.

A bad guy has a fairly simple motivation. He wants power and the freedom to exercise that power, although the antagonist would call it "defending his own interests." These are the kinds of books that have a CIA spy versus an evil dictator, or an exiled king versus a pretender to the throne, or an FBI agent versus a serial killer.

In *The Silence of the Lambs,* Hannibal Lecter wants to escape from prison so he can kill more people. Being in prison is messing up that grand plan. He wants to use the heroine, who is a naive FBI trainee, as his way out, and he thinks nothing of killing prison guards or torturing innocent bystanders in order to free himself.

The temptation is to make the bad guy simply evil, full stop. However, it's important to make these kinds of villains three dimensional. Give us some hints that show us the antagonist's true motives, and how they took such a wrong turn in life.

Nine times out of ten, the hero in these stories must kill the bad guy. A bad guy is so ruthless, and so unstoppable, that if the hero doesn't end him once and for all, he's going to give it another shot. Sometimes the hero can overpower the bad guys, imprison them, or expose them for what they truly are, but for this particular kind of antagonist, it usually ends in death.

Rival

A rival is the antagonist who's competing for the same prize as the protagonist. It could be a professional rival going after the same job or promotion. It could be a sports rival playing for the opposing team. It could be a political rival trying to get elected to the same office. Or it could be a romantic rival who's trying to win the girl or the guy in a love triangle situation. This dynamic can be found in sports books, literary fiction, comedies, and young adult fiction.

In these stories, the protagonist and the antagonist both want the same prize, and they're both working equally hard for it. They respect each other's accomplishments, and if circumstances were slightly different, the two of them would probably be friends. Even so, you're going to make it so readers root for the hero and hate the rival because the rival is arrogant. The rival boasts, he brags, and he takes pleasure in the hero losing. He has eyes only for the trophy, and will do anything to get it. He's not interested in emotional growth along the way. After all, he already thinks he's the best.

If your story has a rival antagonist, remember that the prize is never just the prize. It's always a symbol for something more. Perhaps your hero needs to beat his rival for a job promotion because he needs to pay past-due child support, and show his children that he can provide for them. Perhaps a girl has been bullied by her nemesis since kindergarten, and now that they're high school seniors, winning class president over her rival would put an end to that childhood trauma once and for all.

In *Legally Blonde* by Amanda Brown, protagonist Elle Woods goes to law school to win back her boyfriend. But when she gets there, he has a new girlfriend named Vivian. Not only is she dating Elle's ex, she's also competing with Elle in law school. Vivian is everything Elle isn't: serious, old money, and on top of the social ladder. Beating Vivian means more than getting her boyfriend back. Elle doesn't need a man so much as she needs acceptance in the sophisticated world of Harvard Law school. Vivian is an obstacle to both of those goals.

Since the rival isn't an evil person, and he's motivated by the same thing the hero is, these stories usually end with the hero winning, then immediately offering a hand in friendship to the rival, or some other gesture of esteem. Don't leave out that moment. Our heroes must be the bigger person. This is why they're our heroes.

When you're revising, think about what the prize in your story symbolizes, and how it would change both the protagonist's and the antagonist's lives if they win it. This will set your story stakes higher, and help you create a rival character who will make a hero out of your protagonist.

Button Pusher

A button pusher is an interesting, complex antagonist. The button pusher has the very best of intentions. Really, they do. In their mind, everything they do is for the hero's own good. The antagonist is wrong about this, or at least they go about it the wrong way, but their intentions are always to help the hero, as misguided as that help is.

You see this kind of villain a lot in young adult fiction, women's fiction, and literary fiction. The button pusher is someone in a position of power over the hero, whether it's a boss, a teacher, or a parent. So the hero can't really escape from the antagonist. The hero has to deal with her. And this person knows the hero, which means she knows the hero's weak spots. She knows exactly where those hot buttons are and she's going to push them over and over until she gets her way.

The button pusher is always eager to share what's wrong with the hero. She finds the protagonist lacking in some respect and wants to fix him. For example, an overbearing mother who thinks she has to speak up for her son on the playground, not trusting him to fight his own battles. Or the teacher who tries to convince a talented kid not to go to music school, but to go into accounting instead, saying, "you're not cut out for the artist's life." I think a lot of us can relate to this dynamic. We all have people in our lives who are trying to mold us into something that we don't want to be—something that the button pusher thinks is ideal, even though it's not what we want.

The Joy Luck Club by Amy Tan is about four Chinese mothers who emigrate to America and raise American daughters. The daughters are the protagonists and the mothers are the antagonists. Each mother is her daughter's button pusher. The mothers try to direct every aspect of their children's lives, even after their daughters are grown. The daughters are tired of dealing with these tradition-bound women from a different generation and a different culture, but every single thing the mothers do is done out of love. Whether it's making their kids play piano, or forcing them to go to Chinese school after regular school gets out, or discouraging them from dating anyone who isn't Chinese, they're trying to protect their daughters from what they see as the worst of American culture.

Dumplin' by Julie Murphy is about a plus-sized teen named Willowdean, whose former beauty queen mother now hosts the beauty pageant she once won. Willowdean decides to enter the pageant, partly as a joke, partly as a protest against unrealistic beauty standards, and partly to scandalize her mother. Willowdean's mother is hard on the teenage contestants, expecting perfection in dress, demeanor, and especially body type. Willowdean's aunt died from complications due to extreme obesity, and Willodean's mother is terrified that her daughter is heading down the same path. Willowdean's mom doesn't see herself as upholding unrealistic beauty standards for women. She sees herself as saving her daughter's life.

It's vital that your reader understands where your fictional button pusher is coming from. By the end of the novel, the hero is going to start looking past the behavior to the true loving motive underneath. Overcoming this kind of antagonist means finding new peace and understanding by reconciling with the button pusher.

Show this reconciliation, don't just tell it. It's not enough for the heroine to forgive her dad, or understand her boss, or accept her grandmother's ways. She has to *do* something to show a change in status. When you're ending your novel with reconciliation, you still need to provide the big, beautiful climax that readers demand.

On the day of the beauty pageant, Willowdean reconciles with her mother when she helps her mother fit into her old pageant gown, and her mom confesses her own struggles with weight. Willowdean finally understands her mother's point of view, and feels completely accepted by her mother, no matter what her body looks like. At the end of *The Joy Luck Club*, the main protagonist travels to her mother's hometown in China, and meets some relatives she didn't know she had. She can finally see where her mother is coming from. Literally.

Romantic Partner

Are you surprised to see a romantic partner on a list of antagonists? The purpose of an antagonist is to shake up the status quo, and to force the hero to change. Looked at through that lens, the two parties who fall in love in a romance novel are both protagonists, but they're also antagonists for one another. The point of a romance novel is that being in this relationship forces both halves of the couple to change for the better.

This dynamic is also found in buddy comedies, middle grade books about friendship, and books about pets like *Marley and Me* by John Grogan. But romance is where this kind of antagonist truly shines.

The primary characteristic of these antagonists is that they're stubborn. They're resisting. They're backing away. They're saying "No, I can't fall in love with this person, because I'll let my guard down, and I'll be forced to change." Their hearts are saying yes, but their heads are saying no, because change is too scary.

In *Part of Your World* by Abby Jimenez, Alexis and Daniel couldn't be more different. She's a doctor from the city. He's a woodcarver from a small town. She's rich, he's poor. She's sophisticated, he's practical. But their relationship forces both of them to grow. Alexis' life looks perfect on the outside, but being with Daniel shows her that she's surrounded by terrible people who don't want the best for her. In the end, she turns down a job her family lined up for her in order to follow her heart. Daniel's self-esteem grows through his relationship with Alexis, and he starts selling his wood art for what it's worth, rather than what he thinks he can get for it.

The romantic partner is different from the love interest that you find in other genres. Love interests are minor characters who influence the plot in minor ways, and we'll discuss them in chapter eight. A romantic partner is the central protagonist as well as the antagonist, and the entire plot *is* the romantic relationship, and how it changes both halves of the couple.

In the end, love always wins. It's not enough for both parties to have a change of heart and realize they belong together. You must show the reader an outward sign of this internal change, otherwise known as a grand gesture. The hero or heroine will do something over the top, something that shows, without a shadow of a doubt, that they are not the same person they were at the beginning of the story. They've set aside their past fears and are ready to commit to the romantic partner with an open heart.

Unpersonified

An antagonist isn't always a person. It can be a place, like Mars in *The Martian* by Andy Weir. It can be an animal like the shark in *Jaws* by Peter Benchley or the dinosaurs in *Jurassic Park* by Michael Crichton. Or it's zombies, or ghosts, or interdimensional beings, like the ones in *Bird Box* by Josh Malerman. These antagonists aren't evil. They're simply acting according to their nature. They can't be reasoned with, or imprisoned, and they're always all-powerful.

This kind of antagonist is a symbol for a larger theme, such as fear of the unknown, or greed, or human arrogance. In *Jurassic Park*, the dinosaurs represent the folly of playing God. In *The Martian*, Mars represents loneliness. In *Bird Box*, the aliens represent the way we mistrust each other. As you're revising, lean into this symbolic connection. Otherwise, your antagonist will seem two-dimensional.

Sometimes heroes can kill the threat, or defeat it, but often, the way to overcome an unpersonified antagonist is to escape from the situation. Mark Watney leaves Mars. Dr. Grant and his friends leave Jurassic Park. *Bird Box* ends with Malorie finding a safe refuge.

You Can't Fight a Concept

Some authors try to push the unpersonified antagonist to its limits by saying that their antagonist is an abstract concept. They might say their heroine is fighting organized religion, or outdated tradition, or corporate greed. If you're writing about fighting a concept then you're no longer writing a novel. You're writing an essay.

Your readers have a strong need to root for the

hero. They have an equally strong need to root against the antagonist. They can't do that if your antagonist is an abstract concept.

The true villain can be an abstract principle, but here's the trick: give your concept a human face. If the real problem is greed, then the antagonist can be the banker who's illegally foreclosing on the hero's farm. If the real problem is outdated tradition, then the antagonist can be a grandfather or some other elderly figure who holds a lot of power in a family. It must be personified in that way. Without a face on your concept, your story will flatline.

Stories rely on moves and countermoves to keep the story progressing forward. An antagonist reacts to a hero's actions by intensifying his opposition. Even an unpersonified antagonist like a hungry dinosaur or a hostile planet can always make things worse. But abstract principles can't, since they're already as bad as they can get.

In *The Hunger Games* by Suzanne Collins, what is Katniss fighting against? She's not really fighting the other contestants in the arena. They barely have names or faces. Her true antagonist is the deliberate cruelty of a fascist government. That concept is personified in President Snow. He's the one who's escalating events behind the scenes. He's the one who's making things worse. He's the one to beat.

Here's the other problem when your antagonist is an abstract concept: how do you know when you've won? Concepts like corporate greed and outdated tradition can't be defeated or overcome. There is no ending there. However, you can convince the traditional grandfather to let you marry a man from a different religion. You can raise enough capital to save the farm and humiliate the banker who tried to take it. This is what gives readers the satisfying ending they crave. There's closure there. At the end of *The Hunger Games* trilogy, Katniss kills President Snow. That's an ending readers can feel.

Confronting the Antagonist

Even though different genres have different expectations for dealing with the antagonist, the protagonist must *directly* confront the antagonist at the climax, in person, up close.

In a thriller, the hero and the bad guy are going to try to kill each other. This is not about the hero stopping the villain's plan, or taking away the villain's power. That's not direct enough. This is about total and utter defeat of the villain at the hands of the protagonist.

If your novel has a rival antagonist, the final competition is going to be one-on-one. The protagonist races against the antagonist. It's not each of them racing against the clock and seeing who has the faster time. It's a head-to-head competition, in public, so their peers know who the victor is.

If your antagonist is a button pusher, then the antagonist and the heroine are going to have it out verbally. The heroine is not going to write a goodbye letter and then move on with her life. Make that confrontation happen face to face. The heroine and her button pusher are going to say some extremely harsh words to one another and keep talking until they come to an understanding.

An unpersonified antagonist is the exception to this rule, since the main way to defeat the monster is to escape from it. However, the heroine always gets her licks in before she runs. She fights hard, in a direct way, and injures the antagonist enough to allow her to escape.

In a romance, the romantic partner is going to make a grand declaration of love. He's going to show how much he's changed for the better. The hero's not going to send an email. He's not going to do it over text. He's not going to have flowers and an apology note delivered. He's going to humble himself, maybe even grovel a bit, to show the heroine his love, face to face. A buddy comedy is much the same, with just as much embarrassment, but a lot less kissing.

A Second Look

1. Which kind of antagonist (bad guy, rival, button pusher, romantic partner, unpersoni-fied) does your story have? Are they the expected antagonist for your genre? If you're not sure, make a list of the top ten books in your genre and the antagonist for each. If your antagonist is not suitable for your genre, think of ways to modify the antagonist to better suit your story, starting a separate document if necessary.

2. Write down what your antagonist wants and the reason behind it. Why does your antagonist believe he's doing the right thing? Have you shown that motivation on the page? If not, brainstorm ways to show that the antagonist thinks of himself as a hero, and mark the places you'll show it in the manuscript.

3. Write down all the ways your antagonist is stronger than your heroine, and all the ways you've shown that in act one. Point to the "Drown the Puppy" scene. If you haven't included that scene, brainstorm ways to show the antagonist flexing his strength and mark the place in the manuscript where that scene will go.

4. Look at the ultimate end of your antagonist. If the scene isn't genre-appropriate, brainstorm a new ending and make notes about how you'll revise your manuscript to put this new ending in place.

FOUR

Turning Points

Being able to write good scenes, even great scenes, is not the same as writing a good novel. If that were the case, I could pick out all my favorite scenes from my favorite novels, splice them together, and call it my new favorite book. But that would be ridiculous, because those scenes wouldn't have a cause-and-effect chain, and wouldn't provoke any kind of emotion in the reader.

You should polish every one of your scenes, but the most important ones are the turning points. These are the big, dramatic scenes that spin the plot in a new direction, and they need to shine.

Many instructors like to break the novel into three acts, but act two is twice as long as acts one and three, so it makes more sense to talk about the four quarters of a novel. At each quarter turn, the plot has a new job to do. As an editor, I always look at the turning points first. These are the foundational scenes, and the scenes that readers will remember most. Fixing these scenes will go a long way toward fixing your entire novel.

The Hook

The best way to start a story is with a scene. Not backstory, not static description, not memories or nostalgia, and not set-up. A scene. There's a time for showing and a time for telling. Chapter one is a time for showing. The hero should be active here, and the scene should use all five senses, body language, thought, and emotion.

Your hero's life is about to change, and your book should start on the cusp of that change. Save the explanation and backstory for later chapters. When readers start a book, they don't want to know what happened before. They want to know what's happening right now. Think about what's a normal day for your hero, and how today is going to be a departure from that norm.

The job of this scene is to introduce the protagonist and his world. The hook has other jobs to do, such as setting the tone and the pace, and some authors like to get the plot humming right on page one, but that's optional. Nothing is as crucial as introducing the hero and his world. You show readers who the hero is by showing them what he does. You show readers your fictional world by letting the hero interact with that world in an active scene.

Readers will pick up your novel and sample just a page or two before deciding if they want to buy it. They're asking themselves, "Do I like this hero? Am I interested enough to spend three hundred pages with him?" You need to give them an interesting character to root for right on page one. You also need to give readers a few hints about the story to come. In chapter one, you're making a promise to the readers. You're saying to them, "Conflict is coming, and it will be the kind of conflict you like."

Killers of a Certain Age by Deanna Raybourn is a thriller about four female assassins who work for a criminal-hunting agency they call the Museum. In chapter one, the heroines are assigned to take out an evil arms dealer. Everything goes wrong, but they improvise a new plan on the spot and get the job done. Then the four assassins parachute off a plane, landing in St. Tropez in the French Riviera.

The heroine, Billie Webster, is quick-thinking, practical, and protective of her crew. It's her bravery and refusal to quit that lets them succeed in their mission. She makes sure her three friends have jumped to safety before leaving the plane herself. In just a few short pages, readers understand who Billie is and what's she's capable of. They know right away that *Killers of a Certain Age* will be full of danger, international settings, and badass heroines.

Plot Point One

Roughly a quarter of the way into the book comes a turning point called plot point one. This is when the heroine is called to adventure, and crosses into a new world. The new world doesn't have to be a new place. It can be a new situation or a new phase of life. In a young adult novel, it might be starting a new school. In a romance, the new world is a brand-new relationship. In a murder mystery, it's the new problem of a murder victim, and suddenly having a bunch of suspects.

This new situation is a definitive break from the heroine's ordinary life. Once she starts down this new path, she can't change her mind. Make sure you haven't given your heroine an easy out. Life is about to get very, very hard for her, so you've got to revise your story to make it impossible for her to quit. She has to see things through.

Your heroine must be active here. You want your protagonist to have agency. You want the story outcome to be in her hands. It's your heroine's decisions and her actions that lead her into act two. The door will slam behind her, but it was her choice to walk through that door.

In *The White Tiger* by Aravind Adiga, this is the moment when Balram decides to become a chauffeur to escape his grandmother's marriage plans for him. In *Legally Blonde* by Amanda Brown, this is the moment when Elle decides to follow her boyfriend to law school in an attempt to win him back. In *The Hobbit* by

J.R.R. Tolkien, this is the moment when Bilbo agrees to help the dwarves retrieve their treasure.

Plot point one isn't something that happens to the heroine. Plot point one is what she decides to do about it. Something has happened to disrupt the heroine's ordinary world. Something life-changing has occurred and now she has a decision to make. Balram had no control over his grandmother's matchmaking. Elle didn't want her boyfriend to break up with her and then leave for Harvard. Bilbo didn't know he would be invited on a quest. However, the protagonists decide to step up and make the next choice, sending the story in a new direction. Balram escapes an arranged marriage by going to work for a rich man. Elle works her butt off to get into law school so she can follow her boyfriend. Bilbo decides to help the dwarves, beginning the adventure of a lifetime. When you're revising, make your first plot point a big departure from everything that came before, and make your heroine actively choose to go for it.

In *Killers of a Certain Age*, Billie Webster grew up with neglectful parents and she's always mad at the world, so she was an easy recruit for the Museum. Now in her sixties, she hasn't mellowed much, and she's uncomfortable with the idea of quitting. She's gritting her teeth through the retirement cruise she's taking with her old team.

At plot point one, Billie discovers that there's a hit out on her team. Billie doesn't trust anyone, not even her employer, so she's not particularly surprised by this development. She turns the tables, and takes out the would-be assassin instead. She is once again on the job, thinking on her feet, and doing whatever it takes to stay alive and finish the assignment—if only she knew what that assignment is.

Billie and her crew blow up the cruise ship, faking their own deaths. They escape by lifeboat and land in St. Kitts. Billie never expected that someone would try to kill her and her friends, but clearly, the Museum found them expendable. She thought she would be floating into an easy retirement, but now she'll have to use all the skills she learned on the job just to stay alive.

The Midpoint

Your hero has walked through the doorway of no return at plot point one. He's doing his best to figure out the rules of this new world you've thrust him into. Then comes the midpoint scene, in the center of your novel, which totally shakes up the narrative.

Give readers everything they want in this center-piece scene. In a thriller, readers want a huge explosion or an epic chase. They want action and danger. In a family drama, readers expect a juicy argument, full of barbs, accusations, and secrets revealed—the kind of argument the neighbors would buy tickets to see. In a contemporary romance, readers expect a hot bedroom scene that brings the relationship to a new level. In a murder mystery, this is where the second murder occurs, showing the reader that a dangerous killer is still out there.

The midpoint scene is filled with action, emotion, and drama. It's full of action, because a lot is happening. It's filled with emotion because the characters care deeply about what's just occurred. It's full of drama because the plot has been abruptly turned in a whole new direction.

Whatever terrible event happened in the first part of the novel has quite suddenly gotten worse. This isn't a gradual realization or an internal thought. This is shit going down, hard and fast, and the hero never saw it coming. In *Jurassic Park*, this is where dinosaurs escape from their cages and start eating people. In *The Wizard of Oz*, this is where Dorothy finally makes it to the Emerald City, but the Wizard demands the Witch's broomstick before he'll send her home. In *Sense and Sensibility*, this is where both Dashwood sisters are betrayed, as Elinor finds out the man she's been spending so much time with is already engaged, and Marianne learns that her boyfriend Willoughby is a scoundrel.

Even though this sudden shift feels shocking to the protagonist, the problems were there all along. Those hungry dinosaurs were already in unsafe cages. The Wizard never had any intention of sending Dorothy home without that broomstick. John Willoughby was always a cad. It's just that the heroine never saw it. She was so busy dealing with the new world she was in that she didn't appreciate the full scope of the situation. The heroine kind of thought her problem would be an easy fix. But good writers never let their heroes solve things the easy way.

When we say the stakes are raised, what we really mean is that the true stakes are *revealed* at the midpoint. There's a context change that happens at the midpoint, and the hero sees what the antagonist is truly capable of. This is where he comes to terms with what he's really up against. This context shift forces the hero to make new choices. In *Jurassic Park*, Dr. Grant must protect two young children while trying to escape an island crawling with hungry dinosaurs. In *The Wizard of Oz*, Dorothy can no longer run away from the Wicked Witch, but must face her directly. In *Sense and Sensibility*, Marianne and Elinor must look elsewhere for love and security.

Take another look at your midpoint scene, and make sure it's a true plot turn. Without that, you'll end up recycling the same conflict over and over, like a bickering old couple who've been having the same fight about loading the dishwasher since 1985. It's really easy to get stuck in that plot churn, where the characters spin their wheels chapter after chapter. Instead, elevate and complicate your main conflict. Make it worse. Make it harder to achieve in less time. Most of all, make it matter more.

There's not just a shift in the plot here, but also a shift in the heroine's internal state. This is the place where she's done running and hiding and making mistakes. She has new information. She has a new perspective. Horrible things have just happened, but she finally has a grasp on the true problem. Now, she's finally ready to go on the offensive.

In *Killers of a Certain Age*, Billie and her crew stumble to a safe house and try to figure out what's going on. They're used to detailed assignments, with everything spelled out for them, not this confusing mess of questions. They're used to the Museum having their backs, and now they don't have any resources.

At the safe house, Billie and her team discard several options before deciding to contact an old colleague for help. The meeting does not go well. It's a huge scene with disguises, traps, backup plans, and a double-cross, as the man they called for help tries to kill them. Billie can't rely on her teammates and has to kill her old colleague herself. Before he dies, he tells Billie why her team is being targeted. The Museum thinks they've gone rogue, and needs to eliminate them.

At the exact middle page of the novel, Billie realizes that the Museum knows where they are, and will never stop hunting them. They have no choice but to go on the offensive. If they don't take out the head of the Museum, their lives will be in danger forever.

The All-Is-Lost Moment

At about the 75% mark of a novel, there comes a moment when the hero thinks he's failed. He's been trying to solve new problems using old methods, and it's been working—up to a point. That point is now, when his old methods stop working and he has a major setback.

This is the all-is-lost moment, when things are as bad as they can be, and the hero almost gives up. This is a character beat, not a plot beat. There won't be much happening on the page other than the hero wallowing. The hero needs to feel all of those negative emotions in order to truly understand that if he doesn't change himself, there's no way for him to win.

This is the moment in *The Wizard of Oz* when Dorothy is locked in the Wicked Witch's castle, certain she'll never see home again. This is the moment in *Dumplin'* when Willowdean has lost the beauty pageant, and any hope of reconciliation with her mother. This is the moment in *The White Tiger* when Balram's employers frame him for a hit-and-run accident, and he understands how thoroughly the deck is stacked against people of his class, and how he'll never work his way out of it.

When you're revising, make sure you haven't skipped over this scene or made it too short. Readers need to feel these feelings right along with the protagonist. In the climax of the novel, the hero will give it one last try, and will defeat the antagonist once and for all, but that victory will be hollow if the hero doesn't experience this low point first. This is an emotional moment, and you should put every one of those emotions on the page.

The all-is-lost moment is where your hero experiences the most growth. Since the midpoint, he's been facing the true antagonist head-on, using all his skills to solve the plot problem. The bad guys, sensing the threat, have become stronger and more ruthless. There hasn't been much time for internal reflection. Besides, the hero didn't think he needed to change himself, and would be quite happy if he could solve this problem without having to go through any kind of transformation.

However, the events of the plot don't give him any choice. If he doesn't change, he'll never win. The all-is-lost moment forces the hero to come to terms with his internal stakes and finally resolve the character flaw that's holding him back.

Bring your hero as low as possible at this moment. Your hero needs to have a true inner reckoning at this point. Revise your story so that your hero has no choice but to change. Without that inner transformation, the final victory won't mean anything. It won't be important or earned, and the reader won't trust that it will stick.

Going through that low moment, facing his biggest fears and shortcomings, and facing the truth about himself, is what finally heals your hero. Only a whole-hearted person is able to defeat the antagonist.

At the all-is-lost moment in *Killers of a Certain Age*, Billie's team has recruited her old lover, who is a fellow member of the Museum. He's stunned that she's still alive, because Billie never bothered to tell him that she didn't die on the blown-up cruise ship. He still cares for her, but they never got together because Billie pushes away everyone in her life. If she doesn't stop that, she's never going to succeed in eliminating the head of the Museum. She needs her team and she needs to trust them.

Their mission is all but impossible, but Billie has new resolve to see it through. She's going to need to use her skills, and her meager resources, and actually rely on her team, trusting that they have her back.

The midpoint gives your heroine clarity as far as the *plot* goes. The all-is-lost moment gives her clarity about *herself*. Now, she knows what she has to do to achieve her goal, and she knows what internal change has to happen in order to succeed. Make sure you've used the all-is-lost moment to give your heroine everything she needs for the big showdown to come.

The Climax and Resolution

The last quarter of the book should be the point where your reader finds it nearly impossible to put your book down. Readers expect an epic climax to a novel, and that's what you should deliver. The climax is the ultimate test. Has your heroine leveled-up? Does she now have what it takes to defeat the antagonist? Has she learned her lessons? Was everything she went through in the plot worth it?

Sometimes the big showdown is a physical fight. The hero has trained for this battle and is finally in a place where he can win it. Sometimes the climax is a reconciliation. The hero has gained new insight into the person who he's been butting heads with, and now has the compassion and understanding to live with this person in harmony.

What's your genre's version of an epic climax? If you've written a thriller, space opera, or high fantasy, it's probably going to involve weapons and death. These genres end with the defeat of the antagonist. However, literary, YA, and romance novels usually don't end in defeat of the antagonist, but instead with the hero and his nemesis finally making peace. If you've written a romance, it's going to be grand declarations of love. If you've written a young adult novel, your climax is going to be your heroine doing something to prove how mature she's become.

No matter what, the climax must solve the central story problem once and for all. The hero has changed through the story, and those changes are what's going to let him overcome all obstacles at the climax. It shouldn't be easy. It should take everything the hero has in him, but your hero has come to a place where he *can* give everything in order to achieve this goal.

When you're revising, check that you haven't jumped directly from the all-is-lost to the climax. In order for your climax scene to feel epic, it needs to build. Your heroine should be gathering her team, gathering resources, and preparing for the final show-down. This isn't just in thrillers or other high-octane books. This happens in a modified version in literary fiction, as the heroine mends the fences she broke along the way, gathering her community around her as she faces her fears and finds her true place in the world. In romance, you'll need a scene where the hero-ine's girlfriends support her and validate her choices right before the final scene of reconciliation and grand declarations of love. In YA fiction, you'll have the heroine finding new confidence, finding ease in her social life and taking a leading role among her peers that she didn't have before.

The heroine is stronger now, but she's still going to need every resource she has in order to achieve her goal. Everything is on the line now and she's not holding anything back. In *The Martian*, the entire planet of Earth is cooperating to bring Mark Watney home. NASA borrows resources from other countries, and Watney's own crew returns to Mars to help rescue him. Watney does a hell of a lot on his own, heroically, but gathering allies was an important part of it.

Killers of a Certain Age builds to a crashing climax,

as Billie and her team prepare to take out the ultimate bad guy who now heads the Museum, a man named Gilchrist. They plan to infiltrate an art auction and remove Gilchrist there, but he sees them coming and kidnaps Billie.

Gilchrist tries to make Billie distrust her team-mates, but thanks to the all-is-lost moment, Billie won't fall for that trap. She and her friends work together to defeat Gilchrist and his henchmen in an epic battle that includes fireworks in potatoes and exploding coffee creamer. Just when it looks like Billie is going to lose, her weakest teammate comes to her aid, proving that her trust wasn't misplaced.

After the climax, there is still one more important scene to write: the resolution. This is the final scene of the book. It shows, once and for all, how your hero has changed. This is also known as the validation scene. Here is your chance to show the reader that this story journey was worth it.

The opening part of your novel showed the hero in his ordinary world. The resolution is where you show the new normal. This is a glimpse into the new-and-improved life that your hero is going to live from now on. He's faced his demons, and won.

Contrast the old world at the start of your novel with the new world at the end. Bring your hero full circle to show how life has changed—and how he's changed for the better.

Mark Watney escapes from Mars, and is no longer

the lonely man he was in act one. Willowdean sees her mother—and beauty pageants—in a new light, as she helps her mother take the stage once again. In *Killers of a Certain Age*, Billie has reunited with the one who got away, and has finally adjusted to the idea of retirement.

Plot Meets Character

If all this seems too plot-heavy for you, you can revise your novel by looking at it through the lens of character. The same plot points still need to happen in the same order, and the story progresses in the exact same way as above, but some authors prefer to focus on the hero's internal state.

In the first quarter, the hero feels like an orphan. He's either literally an orphan, or he's without guidance from elders in his life, and he doesn't feel like he fits into the world he was born into. In the second quarter, he becomes a wanderer. He's thrust into a new situation, and has to figure out the rules of this new world. In the third quarter, he becomes a warrior. After the change at the midpoint, he has new clarity about the stakes. He's ready to fight for what he wants. In the fourth quarter, he becomes a martyr. This quarter is all about sacrifice. Either the hero finds the stakes so high that he can't achieve them without risking his life, or he's willing to sacrifice something else to get what he wants, like his dignity, or his ambition, or his freedom.

I want to take a moment to point out that these

definitions are for *the author*. They're not for the reader. You can't be obvious here. You would never have your hero saying, "Oh, I feel like such an orphan." Or, "I feel like a wanderer right now." The four phases are universal, from book to book, but it doesn't mean it's explicit —not for the reader and not for the hero. If you do your job well, the reader will feel those feelings along with the hero, even though you've been subtle about it. Put your hero in orphan-like situations, or wanderer-like situations, and then let the story unfold naturally. Your reader will get it.

In the big turning point scenes, the hero will move from one internal state to another—an orphan to a wanderer, or from a warrior to a martyr. These are huge emotional transformations as well as big plot points. When you're revising, look for ways to make the big turning points mean more to the internal life of the protagonist.

The Orphan

In act one, the hero's mental state is that of an orphan. It's amazing how often literal orphans show up in novels. But even if the hero has parents, he's often without guidance, rudderless, not sure where he fits in the world.

The orphan-state protagonist feels unfulfilled but doesn't know why. He longs for something more out of life, but isn't prepared to get it. He doesn't see any need to shake up the status quo, or feels that it would be futile to do so. An orphan is stuck. He's surviving, but not thriving.

Act one shows us what the hero's everyday life is like, even though he doesn't feel like he quite belongs in his world. Readers need to know all of these normal life details so they can see how much the character changes at the end of the story.

Plot point one marks the hero's transition from orphan to wanderer. For the first time, he's faced with a choice. He can go through the doorway of no return, or stay stagnant and unfulfilled in his ordinary world.

In *The Hunger Games* by Suzanne Collins, Katniss Everdeen is basically an orphan. Her dad is dead, and her mom is too depressed to care for Katniss and her sister. Katniss has been the family breadwinner since age twelve. She hunts in the nearby woods and sells the game she kills to support her family. She doesn't fit in with her peers, and only has one true friend. She hates the cruel government of Panem, but feels powerless to do anything about it.

Everything changes for Katniss at the reaping. Every year, twenty-four teenagers are chosen for the hunger games, where they will fight to the death on live TV as a spectacle for the wealthy. Katniss is devastated when her little sister's name is drawn. Her sister is only twelve, and can't hunt or fight.

It's here that Katniss makes a decision that will change her life forever. She volunteers to take her sister's place. She's no longer acting as an orphan. For once, she knows exactly what she has to do, and she's filled with purpose. Keeping her sister alive is all that matters, and she'll do anything to make that happen, even if it means becoming a contestant in the games. She doesn't know everything that entails, and she's about to enter her wanderer phase where nothing makes sense, but for this one moment in time, she has true clarity and a determination to see things through.

The Wanderer

This section of the book is all about your hero feeling like a fish out of water. He's in a new situation, with new problems, and has to deal with new people. Your hero is trying to figure out how this new world works, but he doesn't have the skills to succeed. He's unprepared physically and emotionally.

Back in the orphan phase, the hero wasn't necessarily happy with his world, but at least he understood the rules there. He knew what he could and couldn't do, and how to get by. Here in the new world, he's trying to find his place without changing himself too much, because heroes are always reluctant to change.

In *The White Tiger* by Aravind Adiga, Balram becomes a live-in servant in a rich man's house. He doesn't know anything about his job, and has to be taught what to do and how to do it. He doesn't know when to speak up and when to be quiet. He doesn't know the basic hygiene standards expected of him. He doesn't know how much money to spend and how much to send back to his family, getting him in trouble with his grandmother.

In *Legally Blonde* by Amanda Brown, Elle is out of her depth in law school. She doesn't understand how to take notes, or how to form a study group. Elle is a California party girl, but her fellow students are all old-money types, and she doesn't understand the social norms of their world. Both Balram and Elle are trying to solve new problems with old methods, but those old methods don't work anymore.

This is also where new characters are introduced, specifically allies and mentors. They provide information, they lend support, and they help the hero find his way in this strange new world. Balram learns from the other servants. Elle makes friends with her manicurist, who helps her feel normal in an abnormal world.

In *The Hunger Games*, after Katniss volunteers, she's immediately put on a train bound for the capital, where she becomes an instant celebrity. She's out of her depth in all of it. She doesn't understand the food or fashion or slang. She doesn't know what to say in interviews, and she doesn't know who to trust. She doesn't have the knowledge or the social skills she needs to survive in this new environment. All she really has is her hunting ability, but when she tries to show off her skill with a bow and arrow during training, she paints a target on her back. When the games begin, Katniss runs away from the other contestants. Her strategy is to hide from them, in the hopes that they'll all kill each other and she'll be the last contestant standing.

However, there's a dramatic shift at midpoint. Six other contestants—including her friend Peeta—have formed an alliance, and they've all teamed up against her. She's caught in a tree while they circle below. This is when Katniss makes her first kill. She drops a nest of poison hornets on her opponents, killing two of them. Shortly after, she kills again, this time in defense of her friend Rue. Katniss is done running and hiding. Now, she's ready to fight.

The Warrior

The Warrior phase is when your protagonist starts acting like the heroine she was always meant to be. Up to this point, your heroine has been reacting to external forces. She's been making mistakes, trying to figure out the new world she's in, and approaching new problems with old ways. But after the revelations and twists at midpoint, she's finally prepared to take some serious action that could lead to real victory. She still has some learning and growing to do, but she's changed enough at this point that she's ready to start facing the obstacles to her goals head on.

The warrior phase often begins with new commitment to the cause. In a mystery, the detective explains to his superiors why he needs to stay on the case. In a romance, the newly committed couple have a date in a public place, letting the community know they're together. In *Killers of a Certain Age*, one of Billie's teammates asks her about regrets, because life as an assassin means making lots of compromises and not living life to the fullest. Another teammate asks her if she ever feels guilty about killing people. Billie replies that she has no regrets, and she's glad she kills scumbags to make the world a safer place.

In the third quarter, the protagonist has become stronger and smarter, but so has the antagonist. The heroine is getting closer to her goal. The antagonist knows this and is working harder to stop the heroine from winning. If he can't go after her directly, he'll start to pick off her allies. The heroine is often alone by the end of the warrior phase.

Although the heroine is stronger now, and more determined, there's still an internal flaw holding her back. Something in her mental or emotional or spiritual world still isn't whole. The all-is-lost moment puts that into sharp focus.

At the end of the warrior phase, the heroine gains clarity on the nature of the internal conflict that she's been waging inside herself, and she accepts her own part in it. She's finally able to admit that the antagonist wasn't the only thing holding her back from winning. It's been her own misguided beliefs that contributed to her mistakes and failures throughout the first three quarters of the story.

In *The Hunger Games*, Katniss teams up with a contestant named Rue who is the same age as her little sister, and they blow up the other team's food supply. When Rue is killed, Katniss recommits to the cause. She vows not only to avenge Rue, but to win the games. Her warrior mindset serves her well, as she no longer has doubt or fear, only determination.

She reunites with Peeta, who is badly injured. When the game-makers tempt her with a backpack full of medicine for him, she wants to go claim it, but Peeta doesn't want her to go, sure it's a trap. It *is* a trap, and Katniss knows it, but she goes anyway, and almost gets killed. She risks her life to save her friend. She has transcended her warrior status and become a martyr.

The Martyr

The martyr phase of the story is when the hero doesn't have anything left to lose. He's fought so hard, for so long, and he's truly willing to leave it all on the field—to win or die trying.

This doesn't have to mean literal death. The life-or-death stakes in your novel can be symbolic death. It could be death of a relationship, a career, social status, or freedom. But the stakes must mean *everything* to the hero. Thanks to the changes at the all-is-lost moment, the hero has new clarity about himself, knows what he's capable of, and knows how to change himself to achieve victory.

Since the stakes are so high, neither party can afford to walk away from the coming conflict. They must see it through. The antagonist is always in a superior position at this point, and sometimes offers the hero an easy way out. In *The Devil Wears Prada*, Andrea's evil boss dangles a job at *The New Yorker* in front of her, tempting her to give in to Miranda Priestly's increasingly unhinged demands. Instead, Andrea quits her job in front of the entire fashion world at a Christian Dior show. The heroine never takes the easy way out, because she's willing to sacrifice everything in order to win—and readers love her for it.

In *The Hunger Games,* Katniss and Peeta fight until they're the only ones left. But now Katniss has a problem. She's come to care deeply about Peeta. How can she kill him?

Peeta volunteers to die first, but she can't let him go. It feels like utter failure. There's no good way to win. The hunger games, like everything else in the country of Panem, is rigged against the poor and powerless.

If they can't win, then they'll have to change the game. Katniss gives Peeta poison berries and they agree to eat a handful of them together, depriving Panem of its victor. It's a bluff, but a dangerous one. What if the government lets them go through with it? But at the last minute, they are ordered to stop, and both are allowed to win the hunger games. Katniss is victorious. It's a bittersweet victory, with a very high cost, but it *is* a victory.

Check Your Pacing

You should study the books you read, because generations of writers have set out good examples for you. As you're reading for pleasure, look at the turning point scenes. They won't be hard to find, just open the book to the 25%, 50%, and 75% marks and see what's on the page. The scenes you're looking for will be there, or nearby. This is an important skill to develop. The more you read with a writer's eye, the easier it gets. Soon it will become second nature, and you'll find yourself anticipating the big midpoint scene, or pausing to appreciate a well-done plot point one.

Killers of a Certain Age and *The Hunger Games* are textbook examples of turning points done well, so they're useful to study. However, you should also notice variations. Why do some genres have a very short act one, thrusting the hero into trouble in the first or second chapter? Why do some authors draw out the all-is-lost moment, letting the hero wallow in misery for pages on end? Why do some authors blow up their midpoint so large that it covers three or more scenes? What effect are these books going for, and do they achieve it?

Go back to the quick outline you made of your novel and focus on the big turning points. Check to see where they occur. Can you divide your book into four quarters? Does one of your sections run too long, and another too short?

You don't have to hit the turning points at exactly 25%, 50%, and 75% of the way through a novel. You have wiggle room. Using the big turning points isn't a formula, it's just the basic pattern for stories in the Western world. You shouldn't break this pattern without a very good reason, but you can bend and stretch the form if it serves your novel. However, if your novel is wildly unbalanced, or if your beta readers say your pacing is off, looking at the placement of your turning points can help you diagnose the problem. Consider the overall flow of your novel. As long as your big turning points are on the page, with your hero changing and growing, you can't go far wrong.

A Second Look

1. Open your manuscript to the 25%, 50% and 75% mark and write down what's on the page. Just a small summary will do. Make sure your big turning points come at the right time. Take a hard look at any acts that are running too long and diagnose any pacing problems. Add, delete, and rearrange scenes as necessary.

2. Look at the hook, or the opening scene of your novel, pointing to the ways you've introduced an interesting heroine on the cusp of change. Point to the places where your scene includes all five senses, thought, and emotion. Make sure you've shown your heroine interacting with her world in an active scene. If you haven't, make a plan to revise the hook to give the reader a heroine to root for and a taste of what's to come.

3. Read through the first quarter of your novel and mark every passage of backstory, world-building, or set-up. Eliminate as much of it as you can, either by minimizing it, pushing it until later, or cutting it completely. Tell readers only what they absolutely must know in the moment.

4. At plot point one, point to the place your hero makes an active choice to step into the story adventure, setting him on a one-way path. If your hero has merely drifted into this new phase of life, brainstorm ways to make his choice an active one, and make sure there's no turning back once the story adventure has begun.

5. Look at your midpoint scene, and make sure it's full of action, emotion, and drama. Look at the big things happening that the heroine cares deeply about, and write down the ways that the story has been spun in a new direction. Write down her context change, and the ways you've revealed what terrible trouble she's in. If these things aren't on the page in sentences you can actually point to, brainstorm ways to raise the stakes by definitively turning your plot in a new direction.

6. Look at the all-is-lost moment, and write down the ways it feels like a true defeat. Write down the ways you've shown the hero's emotion on the page. Write down the exact way this forces the hero to face the fact that if he doesn't change, he'll never win. If this moment is incomplete or missing, brainstorm ways to bring your hero as low as he can possibly go.

7. Look at your climax scene, and write down the ways it builds to a high point, starting with the hero gathering his resources and ending with a face-to-face showdown. Make sure the ending is definitive and that you've shown how the hero has been transformed by this experience. If it's not on the page or is incomplete, brainstorm ways to make your climax more epic.

8. Point to the ways your hero feels like an orphan in the first quarter of your novel. If you can't find any specific passages, rethink your first quarter. Brainstorm ways to make your protagonist feel unfulfilled, or like an outsider, or in need of guidance, and put that on the page.

9. Point to the ways your heroine feels like a wanderer in the second quarter of your novel. Point to places that contrast your heroine's old world and her new one. Point to her mistakes and mark the ways the believer and doubter characters pull her in opposite directions. If any of those components are missing or incomplete, rethink the second quarter. Brainstorm ways to make your heroine feel like a true fish out of water, and put that on the page.

10. Point to the ways your hero feels like a warrior in the third quarter of your novel. Show how your midpoint turn forced your hero to face the life-or-death stakes. Point to the place the hero has recommitted to the cause. Point to the places the antagonist has stepped up his game, making the hero fight harder. Point to the places the hero is sliding ever downward, toward the all-is-lost moment. If any of those components are missing or incomplete, rethink the third quarter. Brainstorm ways to make your hero's fight a worthy one, and put that on the page.

11. Point to the ways your heroine feels like a martyr in the fourth quarter of your novel. Point to the ways the all-is-lost moment has given her new clarity, with a new way to win. Point to the place she decides to sacrifice everything in order to do so. If any of those components are missing or incomplete, rethink the fourth quarter. Brainstorm ways to make the victory more fulfilling by having a changed heroine willing to fight to the death.

FIVE

Story Stakes

In my editing career, I've seen hundreds of manuscripts in all stages of development. The most common problem that I see is that the story stakes are unclear or not developed. Readers need to know exactly what the hero is trying to do, and what happens if he fails. If the stakes are unclear, or they don't seem important, readers won't finish the book— and they won't buy your next one either.

Once readers are clear on the hero's goal, and what he has to lose, they're all in. If you've written a hero that readers care about, they want him to be happy, and they'll finish the story to see if he reaches his goal or not. Knowing what's at stake makes characterization stronger, plots tighter, and emotions deeper. A novel with high stakes, developed in a meaningful way, is a novel that readers can't put down.

I feel so passionate about this topic that I wrote an

entire book called *Raise the Stakes*. If you want to take a deep dive into writing effective story stakes in all genres, that's the book to read next.

External Stakes

When we think of story stakes, we most often think of the external stakes. We love to see a focused protagonist fighting against all odds to achieve a worthy goal, whether that's a knight overthrowing an evil king or a girl stopping her little brother from breaking her crayons. External stakes are the flesh and bones of your story. They're what makes your plot run.

In 1989, Tom Clancy wrote a spy thriller called *Clear and Present Danger*, which is the best title for a thriller I've ever seen. He might as well have called it *This Book has Stakes*, because the title pinpoints what makes story stakes work. The external stakes in a novel have to be clear, they have to be present, and they have to be dangerous.

Clear

External stakes are tangible things the protagonist wants to achieve, like winning a championship, defeating an evil wizard, finding a lost child, or mending a broken relationship. These are stakes that everyone can see, and they either happen or they don't. If someone wins the championship, there's a trophy to display and a title in the record books to point to. If someone defeats an evil wizard, we can watch the wizard fall from a high tower to his death, and see the kingdom renewed. External stakes are concrete, not abstract.

In *Pride and Prejudice* by Jane Austen, Lizzie Bennet and her sisters need to get married to secure their livelihood, since they won't be inheriting any wealth. The stakes are abundantly clear, from the local gossip, to the numerous balls and parties designed to throw young people together, to the matchmaking by Lizzie's mother. Readers know when Lizzie achieves her goal, as they can see the marriage proposal and acceptance on the page.

In *The Lord of the Rings* by J.R.R. Tolkien, a hobbit named Frodo must throw a cursed ring into Mount Doom, otherwise the entire kingdom will fall under the rule of an evil warlord. It takes three thick books and several side quests to achieve this goal, but the reader understands what Frodo must do and never doubts what will happen if he fails. At the climax, readers see the ring melting in the lava fires of Mount Doom, and they know that the kingdom has been saved.

The stakes have to be clear to both the protagonist and the reader. When I'm editing, I see many manuscripts where the stakes aren't spelled out. Writers don't want to be obvious, or talk down to the reader, so they don't mention the stakes at all, hoping the reader will figure them out. However, the time to be subtle is when you're dealing with *internal* stakes. The external stakes should be glaringly obvious on the page. When you're revising, put the hero's goal on the page. You can state it in dialogue. You can put it in the middle of an argument. You can put it in the exposition, telling the reader directly. But whatever you do, make sure your hero knows exactly what he wants, and has some idea how to achieve it. Make sure the reader knows it too.

Present

The stakes are what's happening right now. The timeline is urgent, with problems that need to be solved immediately. If your hero has all the time in the world to accomplish his goal, then it's not really a goal. It's more like a dream or a wish.

In *The Martian,* Watney has to figure out how to grow food and make water in order to survive on Mars. He has to do it right away, before he starves to death. In *Where the Crawdads Sing* by Delia Owens, Kya has to take care of herself from the age of seven. She has to cook her own food and take care of the house, then find a way to earn money for more food, because she has no parents and there is no help coming from the townspeople.

In *Mexican Gothic*, Noemi is trapped in her cousin's house, and can't leave without facing the evil that lurks inside. In *Bird Box*, Malorie has been waiting years for her chance to flee to safety. Once she and her children board a rowboat and start down the river, she can't go home again. There's no plan B in fiction.

Whatever your hero is trying to do, this is his *one* chance, and there's a definite deadline attached. This is easy to see in genre fiction. In thrillers, the hero must save the world before the bad guy destroys it. In mysteries, the detective must find the killer before he kills again.

Writers of literary, historical, young adult, or romance fiction sometimes have trouble giving their stories a ticking clock, but there's always a way to do it. Lots of events have deadlines attached—college applications, medical diagnoses, athletic competitions, immigrating to a new country, even marriage proposals, as in *Pride and Prejudice*. Look at *your* novel and make sure that this is your hero's one chance to change his life, and that he has a limited amount of time to get it done.

Danger

You don't have to write a thriller where the fate of the world is at stake. In some genres, the stakes are bringing an estranged family back together or finding true love. But no matter what's at stake in your story, it needs to be the number one problem in your hero's life right now, with terrible consequences for failure.

If your hero can fail at his goal, and then return to

his ordinary life not much worse for wear, then you need to rethink your story. Consequences for failure must be so bad that if the hero fails, he'll be worse off than when the story began.

In *Lessons in Chemistry*, Elizabeth is a single mom at a time when single motherhood was a scandal. She's willing to put up with terrible treatment at work because she needs this job to provide for herself and her daughter. When she gets fired from her lab, she takes what she considers a humiliating job as a TV chef, because it's the only alternative open to her.

In *The Stranger* by Harlan Coben, Adam Price thinks he's living the American dream in a preppy New Jersey suburb, with a good job, a loving wife, and two thriving sons. That is, until a stranger approaches him with a terrible secret about his wife, who disappears the next day. Price begins by simply wanting to find his wife and reconcile with her. But his questions lead him to danger that is bigger—and closer to home—than he thought possible. Suddenly Price is not only missing his wife, he's accused of her murder. If he doesn't find her, his entire life will be shattered.

When you think about the stakes of your story, don't just think about rewards for victory, think about consequences for failure. Not only is your heroine striving for her goals, but she can't stop striving, no matter what. The consequences are too dire.

The consequences for failure must be death. Every novel. Every time. It either has to be literal death or something that *feels* like death. It could be death of a career, or death of freedom, or death of a relationship, or death of a sense of self.

In some stories, death is absolutely on the line. In those books, the hero either wins or he dies. In *The Martian*, Watney is either going to leave Mars or die trying. In *Where the Crawdads Sing*, Kya is either going to learn to fend for herself or starve.

In some stories, the life-or-death consequences are emotional or metaphorical. In *Lessons in Chemistry,* Elizabeth won't die if she's fired. However, she suffers loss of a career, and loss of a sense of self. In the lab, she's constantly mistaken for a secretary or an assistant, and she's constantly correcting people, telling them, "I'm a *scientist.*" When she's fired, that self-definition dies. She has to ask herself, if I'm not a scientist, what am I? She tries to regain this sense of self when she's cooking on TV, as she treats every recipe like a science experiment, much to the delight of her audience.

The bigger the consequences for failure, the higher the stakes. Those life-or-death circumstances will make the readers worry, will make them concerned for your hero, and will make them turn page after page right up to the end of the novel. As you're revising, check to make sure that the stakes in your story feel like life or death to your hero, and that failure is definitely a possibility. The external stakes need to be nothing less.

Don't Tip Your Hand Too Soon

Some writers try to get the big, main conflict going right away, within a chapter or two. They make their heroes eager to fight the antagonist, consequences be damned, even at the cost of their own lives. But that's what video game characters do. In games, the point is to jump in, fight hard, and win big. Novels are different. We expect our novel heroes to act like real human beings, and real humans hate risk.

No hero wants the external stakes of the novel to happen to him. No hero seeks out that kind of danger. This is the worst-case scenario. Mark Watney never wanted to be stranded on Mars. Elizabeth Zott never wanted to be fired from her laboratory job. Lizzie Bennet didn't want to be forced to compete on the marriage market just to keep a roof over her head. Frodo Baggins never wanted to be in charge of a cursed ring.

Even in a romance novel, with the potential for a lasting love match, the prospect seems scary at first. A new relationship will turn the hero and heroine's lives upside down, and both of them know it. In *Part of Your World* by Abby Jimenez, Alexis and Daniel are both terrified of getting involved, since they come from different backgrounds, live in different cities, and have vastly different lifestyles. They're both going to have to change, and change is always the last thing protagonists want to do.

Because the external stakes are so huge and

dangerous, and not something that a hero jumps into willingly, you'll reserve the big reveal for the midpoint. It's only after the midpoint that the hero understands the life-or-death consequences of the external stakes. Before that, you'll get the hero involved with the story using smaller, more personal stakes.

In *The Stranger*, Adam Price never wanted his life to be upended. To him, the disappearance of his wife is a worst-case scenario. But these personal stakes lead him to the even bigger stakes of blackmail, a murder accusation, and threats to his life.

In *The Wizard of Oz*, Dorothy didn't want to land in the magical land of Oz. But now that she's here, she thinks it's a fairly simple task to get home again. She simply has to take a nice walk to the Emerald City and ask the Wizard. She has no idea that the Wizard will give her the impossible task of bringing him the Wicked Witch's broomstick, and now her quest to go home has turned deadly.

It's only after the hero is in too deep that he realizes what he's *really* up against. That midpoint turn spins the story in a new direction, as the hero finds out how formidable his enemy is, and how much trouble he's really in.

Make your external stakes huge and life-changing. Make them urgent and personal. Just be sure you've let them build, so that the midpoint drama hits just right.

Internal Stakes

If the external stakes are the flesh and bones of your story, the internal stakes are its heart and soul. The external stakes make the plot, but the internal stakes give the readers a reason to care.

The internal stakes represent what the protagonist is missing deep inside at the start of the story. You can't see the internal stakes, but the hero feels them every day. He's lacking something mentally, emotionally, or spiritually, and until he goes through the events of the story journey, he won't be whole. On the flip side, it's this missing piece of his psyche that prevents the hero from solving his story problem on page one. He's too broken to achieve his goal.

This missing piece always has roots in the hero's past. Is he cowardly due to past failures? Does he have low self-esteem due to an abusive parent? Has he closed off his heart because of a bad relationship? Unless this internal wound is overcome, the hero won't win the big showdown at the climax, and he'll never achieve lasting happiness. The cowardly hero must become brave. The hero with low self-esteem must recover a sense of self. The untrusting partner must open his heart.

Primal

You can see and touch the external stakes, but the internal stakes are things like overcoming the loss of a parent, or finally feeling security after years of poverty, or finding self-confidence again after losing your job. Internal stakes are described with abstract words like love, safety, courage, or belonging.

In *The Stranger*, Adam Price's internal stakes are his sense of self-worth. He prides himself on being a family man, living the ideal suburban dad life. When terrible secrets begin to come out, Adam starts to question everything about his so-called perfect life.

In *A Christmas Carol* by Charles Dickens, Ebenezer Scrooge's internal stakes are his loneliness and lack of love. He thinks that money will bring him happiness, but what he truly needs is connection with others.

In *The DaVinci Code* by Dan Brown, college professor Robert Langdon sees everything through logic and intelligence. It's what allows him to solve the world's hardest puzzles as he and his companion chase down the Holy Grail. However, what's missing is Langdon's spiritual life. He's made no room in his life for anything that he can't see or touch, and there's no feminine presence in his life at all. It's only by coming to terms with the divine feminine that he becomes whole.

Self-worth. Love. Spiritual life. These are primal needs that everyone has. Internal stakes are so relatable because they're part of what makes us human. When you're revising, look for the deep, universal need at the core of your hero, putting that human drive at the center of who he is.

Subtle

When it comes to external stakes, the author should present them clearly and directly. However, internal stakes require a different approach. If you state your hero's internal stakes outright, it will be heavy-handed and preachy. Instead, you should subtly weave them into the story, encouraging the reader to uncover the hero's internal struggles.

The hero knows what he wants, but he doesn't know what he truly needs. These needs simmer beneath the surface throughout the story, unspoken and buried so deep that even the hero doesn't recognize them anymore. This blind spot drives his behavior and decisions.

The hero isn't consciously aware of these internal stakes, and the author doesn't ever state them in so many words. The internal conflict only becomes apparent through the hero's behavior. You make the reader aware of them by showing, not telling.

Pretend you're writing a novel about a heroine who never gets attached to anyone. She grew up in the foster care system and now, as an adult, doesn't feel like she belongs anywhere. You wouldn't *tell* the reader that your heroine has this flaw. You'd *show* it by having her sabotage relationships to avoid being left behind, and never fully unpacking her belongings after a move, and teasing one of her co-workers for being "so settled." You'd give your heroine a job that involved lots of travel, and she wouldn't allow herself to get a pet because pets really tie a person down. You might include flashbacks to times when she was moved from one foster home to another, hoping she'd get lucky this time and actually find a permanent home.

If she meets a man who wants to marry her and move to the suburbs, the reader will immediately see why that won't work for her, because you've shown them a heroine who doesn't feel entitled to a home. The reader gets it, but the heroine doesn't, at least not yet. In the heroine's mind, it's not that she doesn't feel entitled to a home, it's that *the world doesn't have a place for her.* Protagonists always justify their own internal issues. In their minds, it's the rest of the world that has a problem, not them.

Sherlock Holmes is the greatest detective of all time. He's so clever and quick-thinking that he can solve the trickiest murder cases before the police even get started. He's dismissive and rude to those he considers his intellectual inferiors, he keeps odd hours, and he doesn't much care if he inconveniences other people. Sherlock is all brains, no feeling. But he's completely unaware of this flaw. In his mind, he's fine. It's the rest of the world that's too slow on the uptake.

In *The Seven Husbands of Evelyn Hugo* by Taylor Jenkins Reid, movie star Evelyn Hugo is chasing fame in the golden age of Hollywood. She dyes her hair blond, changes her name, lies about her age, and uses anyone and everyone in order to get ahead. She enters into strategic alliances rather than relationships.

Friends, lovers, and husbands are for cultivating and discarding according to the needs of the moment. To Evelyn, it's all one big performance. She's constantly hounded by paparazzi and gossip magazines, and playing to them is as important as playing any part in a movie. Evelyn doesn't see this as a problem, or see a distinction between life and the movies. To her, it's all the same show.

Plots Cause Character Growth

Your heroine has been living with her flaw for so long, and has built such strong coping mechanisms around it, that she can't even see it anymore. She's buried it so deep, she has no idea how it's hurting her. If the events of your story never happened to her, there would be no need to excavate it. She would live her life denying this internal need forever. Only the events of the plot make her come to terms with it. Everything that happens in the plot brings this inner turmoil to the surface. In other words, plots cause character growth.

The Case of the Missing Marquess by Nancy Springer is about Enola Holmes, Sherlock Holmes' fourteen-year-old sister. She shares the Holmes family's intelligence, but she grew up sheltered, home-schooled by her mother on a country estate. She knows nothing about the wider world, especially how terrible it is for women. When her mother goes missing, Enola sets out for London to find her, only to be surprised again and again by the way she's treated. The events of the plot force her to face her innocence and grow up, to engage the world as it is, not the way she wishes it could be.

If Enola's mother had never gone missing, she would have happily lived many more years on her beloved estate, perhaps taking over the running of it from her mother. She would enjoy the life of the mind, untroubled by anything beyond her country village, unaware that this was a stunted life. It's only the events of the plot that bring her the growth she needs.

In *The White Tiger* by Aravind Adiga, Balram lives at the bottom of the income ladder, but he's determined to work his way out of poverty. The harder he works, the more his employers exploit him. Still, he carries doggedly on, fixed in the belief that he can climb the social ladder one rung at a time, despite his lack of inherited wealth. When his boss tries to frame him for a hit-and-run accident, Balram realizes that no matter how hard he works, he can't compete with people who have unlimited wealth and great power, and he'll have to escape poverty through other means.

If his boss hadn't run over someone and tried to pin it on Balram, he would have kept working for pennies, convinced that one more year of service or one more favor for his boss would give him the financial security he needed. Only the events of the plot force him to face the truth about his circumstances.

The external stakes are brand-new and need to be

dealt with right now. However, the internal stakes are scars from old wounds your protagonist has carried for years. Confronting those long-standing issues requires him to change, and nobody wants to change themselves. Does your hero *need* to change? Absolutely. But that doesn't mean he wants to. Keep this in mind as you're revising. Your plot must be tailor-made to force that internal change that your hero desperately needs.

Internal Stakes + External Stakes = Story

A good novel has dynamic tension between the external stakes and the internal stakes all the way through the story. The heroine's external stakes, her *want,* is pushing her forward, while the internal stakes, her *need*, is holding her back. The external goal is clear, present, and dangerous, so failure is not an option. At the same time, the internal stakes fill her with fear. The heroine has been compensating for these deep-seated issues her whole life, when suddenly, the external stakes threaten to open that wound. No wonder she's stuck.

This push-and-pull dynamic forms much of the conflict in the novel. The heroine's external world has changed. She tries to fix her problems using her old tried-and-true coping methods, which only makes things worse, so she tries something else, which also fails, because she hasn't yet changed internally enough to achieve her goal. Look at the middle of your novel and make sure you've shown this struggle in every chapter.

In *The Seven Husbands of Evelyn Hugo*, Evelyn wants to be more than an actress. She wants to be the most famous person in Hollywood, and she'll work with, blackmail, or sleep with whoever it takes to achieve that. But deep down, what she really wants is to be loved. She finally finds true love with an actress named Celia, but in the 1950s, to be gay or bisexual was to lose everything. She tries to stay closeted with Celia, but the more Evelyn chases fame, the more their relationship suffers. Evelyn can't have both an intensely public life and a huge secret. She often promises Celia that she'll do one last movie and then retire, but she never does.

Everything comes to a point at the all-is-lost moment. This is where the internal stakes and the external stakes collide. The disconnect between wants and needs finally becomes apparent to the heroine, and she realizes that the only way to succeed is to change herself.

In *The Seven Husbands of Evelyn Hugo*, it's not until Evelyn loses everything—her career, fame, and Celia —that she realizes what the relentless pursuit of fame has cost her. Only when she hits rock bottom does she finally change. She gives up acting to retire with Celia and nurse her through cancer. She finds true happiness, not as a performance, but as honest emotion.

Most modern popular fiction follows this story

structure, but this isn't always true for some kinds of literary fiction, grimdark fantasy, or the middle book of a trilogy. Instead of learning and growing, you sometimes have a hero who knows he has to change, but refuses to do so. In these cases, the all-is-lost moment is inverted to be a false victory, where the hero thinks he's gotten everything he wanted, only to be followed by a crashing defeat.

However, for the most part, readers expect heroes to learn and grow. They love to see their beloved heroes change for the better, becoming better people through the story journey, and ending up happier as a result.

Stakes in a Series

Maybe you've written a trilogy, or you're planning a long series. Maybe you've got a mystery series where the detective solves case after case, or you're working on an epic fantasy that's going to take three books to do justice to the story. You want to resolve each book enough so the reader feels satisfied, but you want to keep the resolution open enough to make readers hungry for more.

In a series, each book needs a distinct plot problem to solve. If you're writing a series, you should lay out fresh external stakes in each book. However, the internal stakes carry over from book to book. Readers enjoy a complete *story* with each book, but it leaves them wanting more from the *characters*.

The Stephanie Plum series by Janet Evanovich has over thirty books in it, starting with *One For the Money*. Stephanie Plum is a misfit bounty hunter who stumbles through her job but always gets her bounty. She's in a love triangle with two handsome men and she's also struggling with adulting. Each of the books ends with Stephanie closing the case and bringing the bad guy of the week to justice. In other words, the external stakes are always resolved at the end of the book. But the internal stakes are ongoing. From book to book, Stephanie has trouble paying her bills, and can't keep a car, and can't commit to a relationship. If Stephanie Plum *does* grow up, if she *does* marry Joe Morelli and settle down, then the series will be over, because everything will be resolved.

Think of it this way: when the external stakes are resolved, the novel is over. When the internal stakes are resolved the series is over. Be sure you *do* resolve those internal stakes in the final book in the series, to give readers the satisfying conclusion they crave.

A Second Look

1. Open your manuscript to the place where the external stakes are clearly spelled out for the reader. If you can't point to the exact place in your manuscript, brainstorm ways to put that on the page, so the external stakes are clear to the reader.

2. Point to the page where it's clear that the stakes are life-or-death. Point to the page where it looks as if failure will be the most likely outcome. If it's not on the page, brainstorm ways to make the stakes matter more, and mark the places these scenes will go in the manuscript.

3. Point to the page where the ticking clock becomes apparent. This is true for all genres, whether directly or indirectly. If there's no ticking clock in your story, brainstorm ways to add one and mark the places in the manuscript where the deadline will become clear.

4. Describe your heroine's inner stakes with a single abstract word, such as freedom or belonging. It must be a primal need that all humans share. If you can't come up with this word, brainstorm a list of words that could

describe your heroine's inner need. Decide what's at stake for your heroine and mark the pages where you'll show (not tell) the heroine's inner stakes.

5. Point to at least three places where the plot forces your hero to grow. If you can't find at least three, then brainstorm ways to put more pressure on your hero to change, and mark places in the manuscript to show it. If you're writing an eternal hero, then show three places where your hero demonstrates that his growth has already happened and he's more than capable of taking on this new challenge. If you're writing an antihero, mark at least three places in the manuscript where he's given the opportunity to change, but doesn't.

SIX

Theme

Humans tell stories to make sense of our world. Every story has lessons about how to live. Theme is the truth about a universal human experience that the author wants us to know. But finding the theme in stories can be tricky. We all have nightmares of high school English when we had to write papers about the theme of *The Great Gatsby* or *The Catcher in the Rye*. And most of our teachers would tell us to write about the novel's theme without ever telling us what a theme actually was or how to find it.

I'm going to tell you the secret that your English teachers never did.

Theme is a Metaphor for the Internal Stakes

When you're trying to find the theme of your novel, look at the stakes. That's where you're going to find it.

The theme of your novel is always hiding in plain sight, buried in the internal stakes. It's difficult for students to find the theme in the novels they read because theme is shown, not told.

In *The Martian* by Andy Weir, the external stakes are Mark Watney trying to get home to Earth. But the internal stakes are Watney dealing with isolation and loneliness. The Martian's theme is human connection and the value of community. In *Pride and Prejudice* by Jane Austen, the external stakes are that the Bennett sisters need to get married to wealthy men who can provide for them. But the internal stakes are that Lizzy needs a man who appreciates her intelligence and wit, and sees her as more than just a pretty face or a suitable match. The theme of *Pride and Prejudice* is seeing beyond outward appearances, and that character matters more than class. In the James Bond novels by Ian Fleming, you'll find themes of duty and sacrifice. James Bond saves the whole world. But he also cuts himself off from the human connection that makes living in the world worth it. The James Bond books assure the reader that it's a sacrifice worth making.

The author never states the theme outright because he doesn't have to. The internal stakes are right there on the page, doing the heavy lifting for him. The reader intuitively understands the theme, as they watch the hero constantly pulled in two directions. That internal struggle tells the reader everything they need to know about the theme of the book.

Theme and Genre

Certain themes are more common in certain genres. YA fiction is about a young person finding his place in the world. Thriller grapples with the question: how far will I go to survive? Horror novels wonder who the *real* monster is here. In romance novels, love conquers all.

The Lightning Thief by Rick Riordan is about a twelve-year-old named Percy Jackson who is half god, half mortal. Zeus' lightning bolt has been stolen and the gods think Percy did it. The external stakes are Percy's quest to find and return the stolen lightning bolt of Zeus before the gods declare all-out war and destroy the earth.

The internal stakes are all about Percy's coming of age and deciding where he belongs in the world. He's the son of Poseidon and a human mother, and he doesn't know if he belongs in the world of Mount Olympus, the human world, or somewhere in between. The theme is understanding your place in the world, and deciding which version of that world is worth fighting for. It's the ideal theme for younger readers.

Get a Life, Chloe Brown by Talia Hibbert is a romance novel about two lovers who couldn't be more different. Chloe is well-off. Redford is struggling. Chloe is a tech marvel. Redford is an artist. Chloe is black. Redford is white. Chloe is disabled. Redford is able-bodied. Chloe is brash. Redford is polite. However, both Chloe and Redford grow throughout the story, through adopting a kitten, a disastrous camping trip, family meddling, and many misunderstandings. In the end, love triumphs over differences, fulfilling the theme.

In *The Stranger*, Adam Price does things he could never imagine doing. In his quest to find his missing wife and clear his own name, he goes from a mild-mannered suburban dad to an armed vigilante. Along the way, he exposes secrets among his peers, dismantling what he thought was his perfect middle-class American life. Thriller readers love reading about protagonists going to extremes, doing whatever it takes to win, especially when the theme is, "family is worth fighting for."

Readers look to their favorite genre to provide the exact emotional experience they're looking for. If your theme is wildly disconnected from your genre, readers will notice. They picked up your novel to feel a certain way, using genre as their guide. Nobody reads a romance novel wanting to feel hopeless. Nobody reads a thriller because they want to feel calm. Nobody reads a grimdark fantasy hoping to feel uplifted. Your genre, story, and theme all have to work together. Take a hard look at your theme. If it doesn't align with your genre, you'll want to revise your novel to bring it more in harmony with reader expectations.

Character Change is Theme Fulfilled

Your hero is going on a journey that pushes him outside his comfort zone and challenges his beliefs. Readers watch him make fear-based decisions over and over, leading to disaster. Only then does your hero change for the better, and when readers see that change, they see the theme fulfilled.

Mark Watney tries to solve his problems by himself at first. But it's only when he gets help from NASA and other space agencies that he's able to find a way home. It's the human connection that he so desperately needs. Lizzie Bennett rejects Mr. Darcy at first, because she can't see beyond his wealth and snobbery. But when she takes the time to actually get to know him, she discovers her perfect match.

In *Dumplin'* by Julie Murphy, Willowdean enters the Miss Bluebonnet beauty pageant as a protest against artificial beauty standards. She wants to force the audience, especially her mother, to acknowledge her plus-sized body as worthy. Her true need—what's at stake internally—is to understand her own inherent worth. She has the wonderful qualities of intelligence, wit, ambition, and empathy. She's a beautiful human, no matter what the world thinks of the way she looks. When she loses the pageant, she comes to understand that her mother always saw her as beautiful, and she can see herself that way too.

If you've written an antihero or an eternal hero, you can also look at a *lack* of character change and decide what that says about your theme. James Bond never changes. But he's weighed his duty to the crown against his loss of humanity and he's decided it's worth it. He's going to stay in the spy game and save the world again.

This is part of what makes a good novel so satisfying to read. We're entertained, we're brought on a journey, and we've learned lessons about life, all without being preached to. Those lessons hidden in plain sight are powerful lessons that stick with us.

Revising for Theme

It's not uncommon for an author to discover her theme while working on her second draft. The first draft is often focused on plot, getting the protagonist to the end of the story journey. Even with a well-developed hero, the internal stakes can sometimes fall to the wayside. However, the second draft is the ideal time to highlight the theme. When you're clear on your hero's internal stakes, and what he truly needs, you've found your theme.

The place to show the reader the theme is in small details. For example, perhaps you've written a novel about two brothers who are on opposite sides of a war, and your theme is the price that families pay for conflict not of their making. In the next draft, you can add smaller details that reflect that theme. Perhaps one of the brothers has two children, and they're always bickering over a toy that they both claim as their own. Perhaps one of the brothers has best friends he considers his found family. He thinks they're more important to him than his real family, because they agree politically. Or he lives over a failing motorcycle repair shop owned by two sisters, and each of the owners blames the other for the business going under, even though the true blame lies with the landlord who has hiked the rent to unsustainable levels, and the city who tore up the road in front of their shop. Always look for small moments that you can use to shine a spotlight on your theme.

In *Legends and Lattes* by Travis Baldree, an orc named Viv gives up the life of a mercenary to open a coffee shop. She starts by buying a run-down stable, intending to renovate it. When the owner expresses surprise that she'd want to buy a stable, Viv tells him, "Things don't have to stay as what they started out as." This is an expression of the story's theme, as Viv learns to trust her found family and becomes a totally new person by the end of the story.

The author could have let Viv take over an existing food-service establishment, one that already had tables and chairs, and perhaps a kitchen. Or, he could have let the stable's property deed pass from one owner to another without remarking on it. However, the author decided to deliberately shine a spotlight on the theme in this small moment.

In *The Seven Husbands of Evelyn Hugo*, Evelyn's first

husband is an electrician for movie sets. She marries him as her first "in" in Hollywood, but she quickly outgrows him when she starts getting cast in movies. Evelyn doesn't blame her husband for their unhappy marriage. She says, "I'd told him I was someone else. And then I started getting angry that he couldn't see who I really was." This small moment seems like just a throwaway line in a chapter about their divorce, but it illustrates the theme. Evelyn is *always* playing a role, not just on movie sets, but in her life. Now, at age seventy-nine, she's looking back and seeing what that role-playing has cost her.

Whatever your theme is on a macro scale, illustrate it on the micro scale. It's almost impossible to go overboard here. Thematic connections should be found in every layer of your novel.

You often can't see these connections until you look at your novel as a whole. Suddenly, the larger theme will come alive in small moments, and small moments can be altered to better fit the theme. It's yet another way the second draft is magic. Not only are you clarifying your plot and deepening your characters, but you're also enriching your theme.

A Second Look

1. Write down the heroine's internal stakes, and the exact way they are appropriate for your genre. If your theme and genre don't match, brainstorm ways to bring your novel into alignment with its genre.

2. Point to five places in your manuscript where your theme is illustrated on a micro scale. If you can't find five places, brainstorm ways to show your larger theme in small moments. This can be in description, dialogue, objects, or relationship dynamics. If you've already got five, consider adding more.

3. Point to the exact place in your manuscript where your hero has the change of heart that will allow him to achieve victory. (Find it at the all-is-lost moment.) Imagine your hero's state of mind ten minutes before this change. Write a paragraph showing his thought and emotion. Now imagine your hero's state of mind ten minutes after this change. Write a paragraph detailing his new outlook. Use material from these two paragraphs when you're revising the scene that shows your character's transformation.

4. Point to three places from quarters one, two, and three where you showed that your heroine is capable of inner change. Now point to a passage in the final quarter that proves that your heroine has changed. If you can't find them, brainstorm ways to show inner change on the page and mark the places where you'll include them in your manuscript.

SEVEN

Voice

———

Readers know what they want for their next book fix and they know where to get it. Watch shoppers in a bookstore. They don't shop the whole store. First, they go to their preferred section. Mystery readers head directly to the mystery section. Romance readers go to the romance shelf. Next, they look at the covers and titles, and read the jacket copy to see if the book aligns with their tastes. Is it the right subgenre? Not just any mystery will do when a reader wants a small-town cozy mystery with an amateur detective. Finally, readers will open the book and read a page or two to see if they like what they see. They'll read a shockingly small sample before deciding whether to buy the book or put it back on the shelf.

What are readers looking for in those opening pages? They're not looking for character or story. You hardly get that from two or three pages. But the reader still knows, instantly, if she wants the book. She's responding to the voice. When readers choose their next book to read, voice is *the* deciding factor in whether a book is chosen. The same can be said for agents and editors, who are proxies for the reader. Some agents and editors don't bother with the query letter, but go directly to the sample pages to decide whether to reject a submission or keep reading.

Readers read novels to have an emotional experience. They're using the words on the page plus their own imagination to get that experience. They need to trust that they're being taken on a worthy story journey with a capable narrator. Voice is how the author assures the reader that they're in good hands.

Voice Is Authenticity

A novel with voice is a novel with confidence and clarity. You've said what you meant to say. You're specific. Your characters have strong opinions about the world and the story they're in. Their emotions ring true.

Open a random page of Ted Chiang's *Story of Your Life*, or Margaret Atwood's *The Handmaid's Tale*, or Stephen King's *Salem's Lot*. These books are filled with strange events, but the description, dialogue, and narrative are so clear that the reader is never left wondering what just happened. The scenes are rich with accurate details, and the reader feels like she's right there. The reader is there because the writer is there. The writer has imagined the scene so thoroughly and recorded it so honestly that the reader is transported.

Especially in this age of AI-written work, you need to be as human as possible. You don't need to be funny, or quirky, or even particularly clever, but you *do* need to be authentic. You need to bring your whole self to the page, without holding anything back.

Voice draws in your ideal readers while simultaneously pushing away readers who are not ideal. Those are both good things. Never try to smooth out your voice or keep yourself in check in hopes of reaching more potential readers. It doesn't work that way. If you try to appeal to everyone, you'll appeal to no one. Write joyfully and fully for readers who like your work. Don't write defensively for readers who aren't your audience.

All Description Is Opinion

Many years ago, I read a mystery novel about a veterinarian. I don't remember the name of the book, but I vividly remember one scene. The veterinarian's young assistant forgot to order the cleaning supplies they needed. This wasn't the first time the assistant messed up at work. The vet scolded her, and the assistant was ashamed, and the author said the assistant, "looked up at her boss through her bangs as if she were a naughty Lhasa Apso."

Later in the same book, the vet meets a man who's strong and confident like a Doberman. She's a vet, so she naturally thinks of dog-like behavior when she meets people. The author was in the heroine's head so much that every bit of description was from her point of view.

But let's say the heroine of your novel is a chef, and her assistant forgot to order the vegetables they're going to cook this week. When the chef is scolding her assistant, you might write, "her assistant's expression fell like an overdone soufflé." An interior decorator might say that her assistant cast her eyes down to the hardwood floors. A businesswoman might say that her assistant's face fell as quickly as the business' bottom line.

It doesn't have to be filtered through your character's job. It could be filtered through her personality or class or upbringing or beliefs. A very whimsical character might say that her assistant deflated like a balloon when she realized she'd screwed up. A practical character might say that her assistant had to know that her screw-up cost the business hundreds of dollars. Someone from Maine might say that when her assistant realized her mistake, her confidence melted like spring snow. Someone from Florida might say that her assistant's confidence blew away like porch furniture in a hurricane.

It's the exact same behavior in every example, but you're describing it completely differently because everything you describe should be the *character's* opinion.

Writers get eager when they're writing their first drafts. They just want to write the story the way they see it unfolding in their heads. But the problem is, writers end up describing things the way *they* see them. It's filtered through the author's experiences and opinions instead of the protagonist's.

That's a problem for the reader, because it gives her a disconnected feeling. The reader is supposed to be sharing the heroine's experience, but she hears the author's voice in her head. It ends up feeling stilted, because the reader doesn't feel connected to the heroine the way she should. Readers don't want to know what *you* think, they want to know what your hero or heroine thinks.

This can creep into your manuscript in subtle ways. I work as an editor and I'm also a parent, so I could easily fall into writing phrases that I would use. If my character needed a fresh start, I might write that she needs to, "turn a new page." Or a situation might be, "as wild as a toddler on birthday cake." Those kinds of phrases come easily to me because they're part of my day-to-day experience. I'm sure you also have similar phrases that come to mind based on your location, occupation, or stage of life.

We don't notice when we're doing this. Those pet

phrases are so much a part of us that when we read them back to ourselves, they sound just right.

But what if I were writing a heroine who isn't a mom/editor? What if she's a twenty-something woman who lives on a ranch in New Mexico and hasn't read a book since high school? Her vocabulary and the metaphors that come easily to her mind will be very different. If she needs a fresh start, she wouldn't need to "turn a new page." Instead, she'd need to "seek out new pastures." Instead of, "as wild as a toddler on birthday cake," she might think something is "as wild as an unbroken horse."

Sometimes you'll get a rejection letter from an agent, or get feedback from your beta readers that says, "I just didn't connect with the heroine." If you get that feedback, this is a big part of the problem. When you're revising at this level, you need to examine every single piece of description and ask yourself, whose opinion is this?

This is your opportunity to sink deep into your characters, to see the story world through their eyes, hear what they hear, and taste what they taste. It's all coming from your imagination, but the trick is to use words and phrases that your hero would use. Whether your book is in first person or close third, you still need to do this.

Think about your protagonist's education level, their background, their age, their gender. Get into your protagonist's point of view, and deliver that fresh perspective to the reader. When you get this right, it makes your description do double duty. You're introducing your readers to your story world as seen through the eyes of your protagonist. Now, all of your description is also character development.

I can't overstate this enough. This, *more than anything else*, gives your book voice. The more you erase the author's opinion and insert the character's opinion, the stronger the voice becomes.

How Much and When?

Description is a signpost telling the reader "look here" and "pay attention to this." The more page time you give something, the more the reader assumes it's important. If you give the same level of detail to everything on the page, then it will all seem equally important, which means that none of it is important. Choose wisely when deciding what to describe.

When you're describing people, places, or objects, pay special attention to things that are new, unusual, or important. Spend more time describing someone the first time they're on the page. Give more detail for key locations, especially if the big turning point scenes will be happening there, but only if it's a place that a reader would be unfamiliar with. Don't go on too long about the corner coffee shop or a suburban kitchen, but do give plenty of detail if it's a logging camp or a panda bear sanctuary or a tiny little house where a pixie lives.

Too little description is also a problem. If readers don't know where to direct their attention, they won't know what they should care about. If the author doesn't describe the heroine's diamond earrings, then readers won't care when the earrings are stolen by her ex-husband. If the author doesn't describe the hero's lucky socks, then readers won't care when he can't play the championship game without them.

Showing and telling don't just happen. A writer uses them to shape the narrative. You deliberately call attention to the important parts of your book by showing. The more important the scene, the slower it should unfold on the page. Look at your book and ask yourself: what do I want to call attention to? What's the most important part? That's where you focus your showing.

Let's say you're writing about two best friends, Ann and Yuki. Both college professors, both moms of young kids, both happily married...until Ann finds out that Yuki is having an affair with her husband. When Ann confronts her friend, readers expect a front-row seat. They want to hear Ann's evidence and Yuki's denial. They want to see Ann's pointed finger, smell Yuki's nervous sweat, and feel the vibrations when Ann slams the door. They want to understand Ann's thoughts. They want to feel all her feelings with her. Show, show, show.

When the fight is over, you don't have to show every move Ann makes for the rest of the day. No need to show her eating lunch, picking the kids up from school, or starting dinner. You can lapse into telling here. "Ann seethed about it for the rest of the day. When Robert got home from work..." After that bit of telling, transition into showing the fight with her husband.

When your last scene ended in one place or time and your next scene opens somewhere else, use telling to orient your reader, then move into the action. For example, "Three weeks later, Josh ran into Sarah at Whole Foods. He couldn't believe how different she looked."

You can also use telling to give a quick sketch of minor characters who aren't important to the plot. "The neighbor across the street was a part-time line cook and a full-time drunk, and wasn't much good at either job. What he seemed best at was sitting on his front porch and commenting on everyone who walked past."

Sometimes, something happens that's so big, the heroine needs an entire scene to process her emotions about it. But if the reaction is small and expected, you can tell it quickly and move on. "Catherine hated the way her co-workers kept interrupting her, and vowed she'd take better control of the meeting next time."

In other words, don't belabor the obvious. Showing is for important stuff, unusual stuff, and the stuff that matters most. Telling is for the less important and more common stuff. Think of showing as a spotlight.

You're shining it on the parts of your narrative you want the reader to focus on, letting the rest of the story fall into shadow. The other parts of your story are still there, but they're not as vivid.

This gets back to the importance of voice and the character's opinion. What does your character notice? How does she express what she's seeing, hearing, or tasting? What language does she use? By choosing what to show and what to tell, you're giving us insight into your heroine. You're not just indicating what's important to the story, but what's important to *her*. If you describe every outfit your heroine wears right down to the socks, the reader will know that she cares very much about her appearance. If you describe lavish meals, the reader will know that food is important to your heroine. Later in the book, if she suddenly starts skipping dinner, the reader will know something is wrong without being told. Showing and telling helps with pacing and can shape the story, but it can also enhance characterization and add greatly to the book's voice.

Get Specific

The best way to bring your authentic voice to the story is to be as specific as possible. Give your readers every chance to stay in the story with your characters by being extremely clear on the page, while cutting filter words, qualifiers, and vague words.

Whenever possible, cut out filter words. These are phrases like, *I saw*, or *I heard*, or *she felt*, or *he noticed*. Using these words is like the author inserting herself between the reader and the character. You could write it like this:

> As Nelson rounded the corner, he noticed three huge men coming toward him. He felt sweat prickle his neck and dampen his underarms when he recognized Zero's assassins. He could hardly believe they'd found him so quickly. He decided to run.

It's far more effective to write it without the filter words.

> As Nelson rounded the corner, three huge men stepped toward him. Sweat prickled his neck and dampened his underarms. Zero's assassins! They'd found him way too quickly. He pivoted and ran through the alley.

The first example hardly gives the reader any emotion at all. Everything is seen from a distance, and the filter words make it seem reported-on and static. However, the second example is in Nelson's voice, up close and inside his experience, with a feeling of immediacy and urgency.

You have to be equally careful about words like *pondered, wondered, remembered, thought about,* or *mused.* Characters think about things, but you don't have to point out that they're thinking.

You could write this: "George pushed an empty playground swing. He remembered pushing his daughter on these swings, and how she always wanted exactly three pushes, no more. He wondered if she still hated him."

It would be far better to write this: "George pushed an empty playground swing. He used to push his daughter on these swings. She always wanted three pushes, no more. That was before she started hating him."

Readers don't have to be told that George is wondering or remembering. They know. In first person or close third-person point of view, readers assume they're reading the protagonist's thoughts on the page.

Watch out for qualifiers such as *seemed like*, or *could be*, or *almost like*, or *as if*. Look for weak adjectives like *nearly, basically, mostly,* or *very.* Also check for vague words like *a little*, *much,* or *something like.* These words rob your writing of its power. Something either is or it isn't. By qualifying statements, you're giving yourself an out. You're saying that it could be like this, but perhaps it's not, or it's only a little bit like this, but not really. Not every statement needs to be definitive, but most of them should be. Since description is opinion, this is the place to let your character's unique world-view shine. The following example uses qualifiers and weak words.

Sharon practically sprinted down the sidewalk, her heels clicking in a way that was almost frantic, but not completely out of control. Her bag felt a little too heavy on her shoulder, pulling her slightly off balance, like she might tip over if she wasn't careful. She wondered if she was actually late, or just almost late, though the difference didn't feel all that important right now.

Here's the same paragraph, edited to remove weak words.

Sharon sprinted down the sidewalk, her heels clicking frantically on the pavement. Her bag dug into her shoulder, pulling her off balance. She concentrated on staying upright. She couldn't afford to be late again. Almost on time didn't cut it. Late was late.

The first example tries to make Sharon's sprint to her meeting feel urgent, but there are so many wishy-washy words that the reader doesn't feel nervous about Sharon's late arrival. The second example is definitive and the reader experiences Sharon's distress along with her. She's late, and it's a problem.

I've compiled a list of filter words, qualifiers, and weak adverbs on my website. Go to AlexKourvo.-com/ForWriters to access it. If you're having trouble with these words, download the list and see how many you can eliminate.

Whenever possible, use concrete words rather than abstract ones. You could say the bar is noisy, or you could say it's crowded with football fans watching the game on the big screens and cheering after every play. You could say that the gelato was tasty, or you could say that the gelato melted into blueberry custard sweetness on her tongue. Remember that one precise sensory detail can stand in for three or four bland adjectives.

You might be surprised at how vulnerable this makes you feel. It's hard to open up your thoughts and feelings to other people, even when doing it through a fictional character. To get around this, writers qualify statements, or use vague terms to distance themselves from strong opinions and give themselves an out. Or they lapse into telling rather than showing, creating more distance. But writers who write in a strong voice don't do this. Their characters know what's what and aren't afraid to say so.

Strong Verbs

Use active verbs whenever possible. Perhaps in your rough draft, you wrote, "There were four chairs in the room, and plants in the window." That's fine for a first draft, but your second draft is a chance to be more evocative, and it starts by using better verbs. How about this instead: "The room overflowed with chairs. Plants crowded the windowsill." Now we've got some opinion. Now we have voice. Or you could go in a different direction if your character likes the coziness of the room. "Four chairs welcomed us to linger, while a variety of houseplants in the window freshened the air."

In your first draft, you could write, "The room was heavy with the scent of abandoned takeout." In your next draft, you could revise it. "The smell of abandoned takeout draped over the room like a suffocating blanket." Or, "The greasy aroma of abandoned takeout curled into every corner and refused to leave." Or perhaps your hero doesn't mind the smell of leftovers, maybe even likes it. In that case, you could say, "The nostalgic scent of yesterday's takeout brought him back to his first college apartment." Sometimes you can't help but use "was" or "were" in your description, but look for places to add more voice by using better verbs.

You can also lend voice by ditching weak adverbs for strong verbs. "The door closed quietly" doesn't have much voice in it, but "the door whispered shut" does. "The door bid a silent goodbye" has even more. The choice of verbs says a lot about your character. Does your heroine see her father walking toward her, or stomping toward her? Does her new neighbor care for her garden, or obsess over it? Does her dog greet her at the door, or does he yap for attention?

When you're revising, adverbs are low-hanging

fruit. Cutting adverbs is a great start. Transforming sentences by adding strong verbs is even better. Using the exact verb that your hero or heroine would use is better yet.

Use All Five Senses

Use all five senses in your descriptions. Too many writers focus on what a place or an object *looks* like, as if sight is the only one of our senses still working.

Back in the day, before movies and television were commonplace, and magazines were only printed in black and white, readers relied on novels to show them places. Distant places they would never travel to were only accessible through books. Having two or three pages of description of a place was considered a feature, not a bug. Likewise, descriptions of clothing and food. Without a book, you wouldn't know that in France, fields of grapes were produced into local wines, or that the markets in India sold bags of bulk spice, or that in parts of America, women were wearing pants so they could ride bicycles.

It's different now. Thanks to movies, TV, and the internet, we can identify pictures of the Taj Mahal, or the St. Louis Arch, or The Sydney Opera House, even if we've never been to any of those places.

Your readership already knows how the world looks, so don't show it to them. Give it to them other ways. When we watch TV, we're only engaging two of our senses: sight and hearing. But books can do so much more. What does Paris smell like? What does India taste like? If you want to know what the French Quarter in New Orleans *looks* like, go there at noon. If you want to know what it *feels* like, visit at midnight.

One of my friends moved from Michigan to New York City, and we kept in touch on social media. I enjoyed reading about his adventures in his new city, as he posted about all the restaurants and shows he went to. After he'd been living there a few months, it got to be summer, and the temperature soared into the nineties every day. One day, his update was a single sentence. He wrote, "In August, New York smells like boiled poop."

I loved that post. It was so evocative. That one sentence made me understand the heat, and the crowding, and the garbage everywhere. I *felt* exactly how uncomfortable it was to be in the city in August in a way I never could with only a visual description.

Characters in Motion

As a general rule, your protagonist should never be standing still, looking at the scenery. She should be touching it, tasting it, or moving through it. There has to be some action involved. Don't describe the coffee shop where your heroine gets coffee every morning. Show her running into the shop, late for work, weaving between the closely packed tables with their mismatched chairs. Show her almost tripping over a stroller parked in the aisle on her way to the counter, where she stands in line behind a woman in yoga clothes, who is staring at the colorful, hand-drawn chalkboard menu but can't seem to make up her mind. In this way, the reader will know that the coffee shop is popular with families. There's a yoga studio nearby. It's a local place, not a sleek chain. That information got to the reader without ever slowing down the action.

Use body sensations wherever you can. Writers are very cerebral, but your characters should be the opposite. Make them as physical as possible. Don't tell us the house was tall. Instead, show your hero standing in front of it and craning his neck to see the roofline. Don't tell us your heroine was sweaty after a workout. Show her wiping sweat off her neck and feeling the grossness of clammy socks as her feet cool. Your hero shouldn't be staring at his new sword, describing it for the reader. Instead, he should be holding the sword to test its balance, noticing how the light glints off it as he turns it, and hearing the whoosh of the air as he takes his first practice swings.

Describing Characters

Some authors refuse to describe their characters, in an effort to make them seem more of an everyman, or to let the reader step into the hero's shoes. This is a mistake. Readers want description. They want to know exactly who this person is so they can visualize him. Readers assign importance to whatever the author spends his words on, so if an author doesn't describe a character, then the reader thinks the character isn't important—which is not what you want them to think about your hero. If you don't adequately describe your characters, your reader won't be able to tell them apart. No reader wants to spend her precious reading time trying to figure out a story where the characters all blend together. She'll get frustrated and move on to another book.

But this is fiction, not a police sketch. It doesn't do any good to tell the reader that your heroine is a tall, underweight girl with straight brown hair. That kind of information needs context. Does your tall heroine slouch because she's insecure about towering over everyone in her class? Or does she walk with her head up, her eyes fixed in the middle distance, because she's training to be a model and she sees her height as an asset? Does she throw her hair up in a ponytail every day because she doesn't want to deal with it, or does she carefully wash and style it before school every morning?

Every heroine has hundreds of characteristics you could share with the reader. Take a moment to think about who your heroine is and what a reader should know about her. Is she ex-military? You could dump half a page of clunky backstory on your reader, or you could say, "her hair was slicked back into a bun as tight as the salutes she used to give." Maybe your heroine is always squinting, like she's sizing up everyone she comes in contact with. Or she's always wrinkling her nose, as if she thinks the world just stinks. The goal is to describe characters in such a way that the reader immediately gets a picture of who they are.

No matter how elegantly you describe a character, sometimes it will feel forced or disruptive to the flow of the story. A good way to make it feel more organic is to use other people in the scene. Compare and contrast for more powerful descriptions.

Say your hero is sitting in class at his prestigious prep school. It's chapter five, and the reader already knows that everyone comes from old money, they all look clean-cut, and they all wear the same uniform. Our hero is talking to the girl next to him, a redhead with a fake tan and fake nails and a fake smile.

In walks the new girl. Her shirt is untucked. Her shoes are scuffed. She has a scar above one eyebrow and chipped nails that suggest she worked her way through life. She's a sharp contrast to our hero's redhead lab partner, who hasn't earned a thing since birth. Come to think of it, neither has he. And he's thinking about it. About her. And you know who else is thinking about this interesting new character? The reader. The reader knows what the new girl looks like, but she also knows how the hero sees her, and a little bit about how he sees himself. Now the reader knows that he wants more from life. He wants to get to know the new girl.

Characters don't exist in a vacuum. They exist in contrast with every other person around them. Your revision is the perfect time to play up those contrasts you've written in your first draft.

Setting is More Than Place

Setting includes geography and weather, but also money, food, religion, gender norms, parenting practices, and so much more. In some genres, setting also includes magic systems, interplanetary travel, or belief in supernatural beings.

You must bring readers into your fictional world, whether the world is as big as an entire kingdom or as small as a neighborhood restaurant. When done well, readers will want to visit your fictional world again and again. We all have comfort reads. When we read these books a second or third time, we're not reading for plot. We know how the story goes. We're reading so we can spend more time in that fictional world.

The Miss Fisher murder mystery books by Kerry Greenwood take place in Melbourne, Australia in the 1920s. The series has everything you'd expect from that setting. Phryne Fisher has a bobbed haircut and bold lipstick. She wears dropped-waist dresses and cloche hats. The men wear wool suits and fedoras. Cars and horse-drawn carriages share the road. There are factories and jazz clubs, lots of drinking, and a great interest in sports.

But there's more to that setting than excellent fashion and good music. A whole lot of young men are missing, because Australia had enormous casualties in WWI. Women are taking up the slack, and working outside the home for wages. They're trying to carefully thread the needle between sexual liberation and a lack of good contraception. There's a huge class divide, causing tension between the haves and the have-nots. Because she remains true to her setting, Kerry Greenwood folds all of this into her stories. Between solving crimes, Phryne tackles issues like drug smuggling, abortion, union rights and aboriginal rights.

When revising, think about what's unique in your setting, and the conflicts that are inherent in the place. Highlight the kinds of clashes that couldn't happen anywhere else.

My favorite technique to describe setting is to make it a problem. If your hero is perfectly happy to interact with your setting in an ordinary way, then your setting will never come alive for the reader. Stories run on conflict. The more problems your setting can cause for your hero, the better.

No one will ever forget the planet Mars from *The Martian*. The entire planet is trying to kill astronaut Mark Watney. The reader understands that there's little air on Mars, and it's brutally cold, and Watney's only living environment is a space tent, and the Earth and home are millions of miles away. The reader feels it vividly because their hero's survival depends on it.

But even smaller conflicts can cement the setting in the reader's mind. In *Where the Crawdads Sing* by Delia Owens, Kya has exactly one day of formal schooling. She's picked up by the truant officer and marched into second grade with the other seven-year-olds, even though she can't read or even count past twenty-nine. She doesn't understand how anything at school works —not the desks, not standing in line, not being indoors all day. But what's most confusing for Kya is the other children. They make fun of her name, and where she lives, and her ignorance. The only reason Kya wanted to go to school at all was for the free lunch, but she's so upset by the other children, she can't eat it. She hides her lunch, brings it home, and feeds it to the seagulls.

People are a problem for Kya. There are unwritten rules for living with other people and she will never understand them. The author had to push Kya out of her comfortable swamp, and into the town—and especially the school—to showcase that. When the setting is a problem for the heroine, the setting comes alive for the reader.

Describing Action

If you're revising one of the big turning points in the book, such as the first plot point or the midpoint, there should be a lot of action happening on the page

—chase scenes, arguments, heartbreak, or first kiss. These big turning points are not the place for a lot of description, setting, or backstory, because those will only slow down the pace. At the quarter marks, you want to speed up. Shorter sentences and shorter paragraphs feel faster. Longer sentences with lots of dependent clauses and big chunky paragraphs seem slower. Check to make sure your sentence length matches the pacing you were going for.

Don't overcomplicate the action you're describing. You want to tell the reader what's going on in the most direct way possible. You don't have to put in every single step of getting your character from point A to point B. Humans all have the same arms and legs and heads and hands, so we know what it's like to walk across a room or drive a car or take a shower, and we don't need it described to us.

Don't explain why your hero does something if it's obvious. If it's something a reasonable human would do, you don't have to spell it out. For example: "The car exploded into a fireball in front of him. Max ran away from the heat and the falling fragments, afraid of getting burned." You don't need the phrase *afraid of getting burned*. Readers know why Max is running. If you tell them why, you're talking down to them. When you're revising, check your description for too much explanation, and find ways to get to the point.

Describing Emotion

Novels are emotion-delivery systems. However, simply telling us about someone's feelings won't have any effect on your reader whatsoever. Words like "happy" or "nervous" don't mean any more to your reader than words like "beans" or "cement." But describing emotion is tricky because our vocabulary is limited to these meaningless labels. Emotion is personal and "nervous" for one person isn't the same as it is for another.

However, there's a way to get around those meaningless labels and make your readers feel the same emotion your heroine does. To show emotion, you need to rely on a combination of physical sensation and thought.

Let's look at a bad example. "Brian felt nervous as he went to the edge of the bungee-diving platform. He was mad at Keenan for talking him into it after one-too-many margaritas, and now he would probably die." This doesn't do much for the reader. We're being told about Brian's emotions instead of feeling them along with him. That's fine for a first draft, but when you're revising, you have a chance to make it better.

You could revise it like this: "As he approached the edge of the bungee-diving platform, Brian's knees quivered, betraying their lack of faith in his ability to stay upright. His fingers, slick with sweat, twitched against the harness as if testing whether they could let go. He couldn't believe he was expected to leap off this flimsy board. Last night, Keenan had plied him with margarita after margarita, telling him he couldn't possibly leave Costa Rica without trying something daring. Now he would probably die."

In this example, we started with the physical sensations, then went to the thoughts behind them. It's best to do it in this order, because that's how humans process emotion. First, we feel it in our bodies, then our thoughts catch up.

Bedroom and Brawling

There are a lot of poorly written sex scenes in novels, but what no one will admit is that the fight scenes are just as bad, if not worse. And they're both bad for the same reason. The author describes what's happening, but only in physical terms. It's all choreography. You're telling readers what body part came into contact with what body part, but they don't know what it means or what anyone is thinking or feeling about it.

Both fight scenes and sex scenes are highly emotional, and if that emotion isn't on the page, the scene will fall flat. Most fight scenes and sex scenes also go on too long. An author will spend two paragraphs on the build-up and then three pages in the bedroom or the boxing ring. Those should be reversed. What the reader is truly interested in is what leads up to the fight, or what leads up to that first kiss. The strongest emotions are in the anticipation, so that's what you should describe most.

Describe the way his hand feels in hers. The touch of his arm around her waist. The way her heart beats in her chest as he gets closer. Linger in her thoughts a bit, wondering if he's going to kiss her goodnight, or if she should kiss him first.

If you're describing a fight about to happen, describe the raised voices, the going up on toes to get a height advantage, the puffing out of chests. Let the reader feel the trickle of sweat sliding down the hero's back and into his butt crack. Show the reader his short breaths, and his racing thoughts as the hero calculates the odds and decides whether to fight or flee.

Once the first punch is thrown, or once the first article of clothing is removed, you've already started to lose tension from the scene. Spend your words where they will have the most impact—in the anticipation.

Genre Considerations

Readers expect different experiences from different genres. They pick up a fast-paced thriller looking for one thing, a quiet literary novel looking for something else. Every genre has expectations and you need to be mindful of them as you're revising your novel.

Thrillers are all about what happens next. What clues are found? What chase scene is happening? Who is in danger? Description of action is highly valued here. In thrillers there is little time for descriptions of emotion or setting. There's no time to discuss feelings when a bomb is about to go off. However, you can still weave in quality description. If your motorcycle chase is set in Amsterdam, describe the cobblestone streets and the row of bicycles lined up in front of the café. Is your heroine scrambling up a mountain after a suspect? Describe her heavy hiking boots and the way her bandana comes unknotted and flaps in her face. Just make sure that the description is part of the action, so the pace doesn't slow.

Science fiction, fantasy, and historical fiction are all about transporting the reader to a new time and place. Description of setting is highly valued in these genres, especially objects that the characters touch, like clothing, money, weapons, food, and transportation. Without adequate descriptions of these objects, readers will be confused. Readers *want* heavy descriptions of the clothing that your eighteenth-century noblewoman is wearing, or the high-tech weapon that your science fiction hero is shooting. The temptation, though, is to do it all in an infodump, going on for pages and pages. If your novel is in one of these description-heavy genres, your descriptions still need to be active. Make your character's opinions sharp, and sprinkle in the description a bit at a time.

Readers of romance and horror are both looking

for vivid description of emotion. Not the *same* emotion, of course. Romance readers want to feel the joy of falling in love. Horror readers want to feel the terror of the unknown. Both genres value description of body language, internal sensations, and emotional states. Readers want to feel what the main character is feeling.

In these genres, your revision will focus on the way your heroine's body responds to story events. Does her heart race? Does she sweat? Do butterflies swirl in her stomach? Describe emotional states: excitement, confusion, fear, dread. What does that *feel* like? Readers want to go along on an emotional journey, so bring them along, not by describing emotions from the outside, but by getting inside your characters and feeling along with them.

Literary fiction values thoughts. The reader wants to know where they are, and they want to know what happens, and they want to feel emotionally about it, but more than anything else, they want to know what the character thinks about it all. What's going through his mind? How is he processing everything that's happening to him? Most literary fiction takes place in the contemporary world, grounded in everyday experience. However, that experience is filtered through a unique character with strong views, expressed elegantly. When you're revising a literary piece, fill your description with unique metaphors and beautiful language. Show the reader the world in a way she's never seen it before.

Every genre needs interesting characters and an exciting plot. Thrillers still need some emotion, romance still needs some thought, and literary novels still need some action. But there's something that each genre values above all. As you're revising, give a little more love to those aspects of your novel by describing them a little more.

All Voice, All the Time

When you're writing with a strong voice, you're being specific and using the character's senses, thoughts, and emotions, which means you're more likely to be showing rather than telling. However, even when you're in telling mode, you can still infuse your prose with unique voice.

Let's say that in your book, Ellen and Stanley are in their kitchen, fighting over who gets custody of the dog in the divorce. The fight gets super nasty and then turns physical. Stanley pulls a knife out of the block. Ellen has to fend him off with a frying pan, taking a cut on the arm before grabbing the dog and fleeing. You've shown all of that in a big, juicy scene.

Now Ellen is on her way to her mom's. It's time for some telling, but it can still sound like Ellen's point of view. Perhaps in your first draft, you had a perfectly suitable transition with some serviceable telling. "Ellen held onto Piper the entire way to her mother's house. When she arrived two hours later, the first thing her mother said was…" We've made the transition from one scene to the next, and we've done it smoothly. However, there isn't anything of Ellen there. That bit of telling could be told by anyone. It could be Morgan Freeman, doing a voiceover.

Add voice. "Ellen kept one hand on the steering wheel and one hand on Piper as she drove. She needed a drink of water, and she needed to check the knife cut on her arm, but she needed the comfort of Piper's downy fur and soft breathing even more. She held onto her dog and kept the speedometer at seventy-five, not stopping until she reached her mother's house two hours later. When she and Piper tumbled out of the car, the first thing her mother said was…"

This sounds like showing, but it's telling. The five senses aren't there and it tells the emotion rather than shows it. But it's telling with voice. We've added specific language and opinion, using words that Ellen would use. That's what readers like. They like strong identification with the character, even in transitions between scenes.

Beware the Betas

I'm a big fan of beta readers and critique groups. However, be wary of any beta or critique partner who tries to strip your voice out of your prose. Or worse yet, tries to rewrite your prose in *their* voice. Voice is the number one thing you have going for you. Don't give that power to someone else.

It's perfectly fair for a beta reader to point out places where you're not being clear. When you see those spots, look for weak words and qualifiers. Chances are, you're going to find them there. This isn't the time to back off, or dull down your prose. This is the time to push forward. Now you know where to add even more voice to your novel by getting super clear, super specific, and super opinionated. Decide exactly what's happening on the page, and exactly how your protagonist feels in the moment, and write that.

Revising for Voice

There's nothing wrong with your rough draft having a bland voice, or an inconsistent voice, or the wrong voice for the work. Perhaps you got caught up in your plot, trying to make all the pieces fit together, and you lost depth. Perhaps you discovered the story as you went along, so the voice at the end doesn't match the voice at the beginning. Perhaps you rethought your heroine, and what was once a cynical single woman is now a big-hearted married mother of five, which requires a different voice. Perhaps you had to rethink where to show and where to tell.

This is where revision really helps you. The second

draft is where you hone your voice by sharpening mushy description and swapping the vague for the specific, filtering it all through a character with strong opinions. The second draft is a chance for your voice to shine. Spend the time it takes to get it right.

A Second Look

I. Write down at least six qualities that define your protagonist. It could be age, class, location, career, disposition, superstitions, pet peeves, or any other characteristic. Brainstorm a list of vocabulary words unique to this heroine. Open your manuscript to three random places and highlight a passage of description. Rewrite it using words that your heroine would use. Make it so distinctive that this observation could only come from this character. Now do it for three more passages of description. Notice how much stronger the book's voice gets each time you do that. Go through the rest of the manuscript and make sure the description is written in your character's voice.

2. Go to AlexKourvo.com/ForWriters to find a list of filter words and qualifiers, (or find other lists online). Refer to the lists for the next two exercises.

3. Search your manuscript for filter words such as *saw, heard, felt*, and similar words. When possible, rewrite those sentences without the filters. Notice how much clearer and stronger those sentences become.

4. Search your manuscript for qualifiers such as *seemed like, kind of, could have been* and similar phrases. When possible, rewrite those sentences without the qualifiers. Notice how much clearer and stronger those sentences become.

5. Search your manuscript for weak adverbs. Replace them with stronger verbs. Challenge yourself to use not just any verb, but the exact verbs your hero would use.

6. Search for a passage of description that relies on sight. Rewrite that passage using the other senses, describing what your heroine is smelling, feeling, hearing, or tasting. Notice the ways it strengthens the passage and makes it more evocative. Use all or part of this new passage in place of the original. Do this for as many descriptive passages as you can.

7. Search your manuscript for words that tell the reader what emotion your hero is feeling, such as angry, frustrated, lonely, happy, or eager. Rewrite those passages to *show* the reader your hero's emotion, starting with his bodily sensation, which leads to thought. Do this throughout the manuscript.

8. Look at transitions between scenes. Keep them short and utilize telling, but infuse that telling with voice by adding specific details and using your heroine's vocabulary.

EIGHT

Minor Characters

Your protagonist doesn't live in the world alone. He's got a family, friends, co-workers, classmates, a significant other, neighbors, a doctor, a dentist, and a favorite barista. All these people add richness to your story and help define your hero. We can tell a lot about a person based on who he chooses to be friends with and also how he treats those around him.

Use your minor characters wisely. It's a mistake to sprinkle minor characters into your novel only to provide realism, or to give your hero friends simply because everyone has friends, or to give him a quirky aunt because quirky aunts are fun. Every character in the story needs a purpose beyond what they bring to the plot. When you're revising, think about what your minor character symbolizes, and play up those attributes.

The Believer

Believers are the hero's main source of support. They provide information, cheerleading, and a shoulder to cry on. It's almost impossible to write a story where the hero doesn't have at least one friend. Humans are social animals and we need each other. Heroes are (usually) likeable, so it's natural that other people will like them. Besides, believers are just plain fun to write. You can give the sidekick quirks that you can't give the hero and she can have all the best lines.

In *The Seven Husbands of Evelyn Hugo*, Evelyn is a movie star who starts out as a poor girl with no connections or acting ability. What she *does* have is a steady friend in producer Harry Cameron. They connect over their honesty and clear-eyed ambition. Harry acts as her sounding board, her matchmaker, her secret-keeper, and her beard. He wants what Evelyn wants—for her to be famous—and he does everything in his power to make it happen.

In the Stephanie Plum series, Stephanie befriends a sex worker named Lula, who starts as her informant and soon becomes her ally and supporter. In later books, Lula works alongside Stephanie. She's always there to back Stephanie up, whether it's chasing a suspect through a rat-infested tunnel or stripping naked to apprehend someone on a nude beach. Even though she gets so scared she needs massive amounts of junk food to console herself, Lula would never miss a chance to ride along.

Because the believer is aligned so closely with the hero's values, he often serves as the hero's moral compass, echoing the hero's beliefs back to him. In *The Hunger Games*, Peeta is the moral center of the book. No matter what, he never wants to lose himself to the corruption of Panem. Even if he has to die, he wants to die with his integrity and innocence intact. Katniss will do whatever it takes to stay alive and win the games, but Peeta reminds her of the cost of doing so.

The Doubter

The doubter also wants the heroine to achieve her goal, but he disagrees about how she should achieve it. Doubters are extremely useful characters. You don't want your heroine to be surrounded by yes-men. You want to give your heroine at least one friend who will challenge her, make her justify her choices, and in some cases, save her from herself. The heroine is going for a big, life-changing goal, and her friends need her to be sure it's worth it.

In the Stephanie Plum books, Stephanie has a doubter named Ranger. A former special forces soldier, Ranger has been working as a bounty hunter for years and is scary good at it. He's supposed to teach Stephanie the ropes, but mostly what he does is try to keep her from getting killed. He starts by buying her a gun and taking her to the shooting range, then tails her as she's trying to find skips, and later plants trackers on her car and in her purse so he can keep tabs on her. He wants her to succeed, but he doubts she can do it on her own. He bails her out of mess after mess, and they both know how much she needs him.

It's important to note that the doubter is an ally of the heroine. He wants what's best for the heroine, but mostly he wants to keep her safe, even if that means holding her back from her goal. In *The Case of the Missing Marquess* by Nancy Springer, both Enola Holmes and her brother Sherlock want to find their missing mother. Enola wants to split up and each search for her, but Sherlock forbids it. It's not safe for a sheltered teenager to go to London on her own. Besides, he's the detective in the family. Sherlock expects Enola to stay at boarding school while he finds their mother by himself.

In many ways, the doubter is a proxy for the reader. If you've done your job right, readers will love your heroine, and it's natural to want to protect people we love from harm. We've all watched scary movies yelling, "Don't go down the basement!" at the screen. The doubter is the character at the top of the stairs, begging the heroine not to take that first step.

The Cautionary Tale

A minor character can also serve as a cautionary tale for the hero. A friend might face similar challenges but make different choices that lead to terrible outcomes. If the hero isn't careful, he could end up in the same boat. It helps if the cautionary tale is someone close to the hero—a sibling, a friend, or a classmate. Using another character as a cautionary tale is a great way to make the hero's potential risks feel more tangible. Instead of having to imagine the consequences of his actions, the hero can see them play out through someone else. Think of Jacob Marley in *A Christmas Carol*, a man who was like Scrooge in every way, and is having a miserable afterlife because of it.

In *The Hunger Games*, only one person from Katniss' home district has ever won the games—a man named Haymitch. He's supposed to be a mentor for the new contestants, teaching them survival skills and helping them strategize, but he's not a mentor at all. He's actually a cautionary tale.

As a teenager, Haymitch was forced to kill other kids, leaving him deeply traumatized. He blunts his pain with alcohol, but no matter how drunk he gets, he isn't allowed to forget. Year after year, he's sent new recruits, knowing there's nothing he can do to help them, and that he's sending them to their deaths.

When Katniss meets Haymitch, she's looking at her possible future. Even if a miracle happens and she wins the games, she won't be a hero. She'll be returning to her district a broken, bitter person with murders on her hands—murders that will haunt her. Unless something changes dramatically, the *best* she can hope for is a terrible life like Haymitch's. If she doesn't want that life, she has to change the system.

When you're revising, look for characters who started out like the hero, but have made different choices, ending up in a bad place. Make the parallels between the hero and the cautionary tale character very clear. Emphasize the similarities in their upbringing, circumstances, opportunities, or worldview. In *The Hunger Games*, Katniss complains to Peeta that Haymitch doesn't like her. Peeta says it's because the two of them are so much alike.

Use your cautionary tale to show how easily the hero could become like that character. Readers will cheer every time the hero makes a better choice.

The Mentor

The mentor character is a source of knowledge, and has unshakable belief in the hero's potential. It's important to note that mentors don't grow and change in the current story. They've *already* experienced their growth, usually in some traumatic and gruesome way, and now they're ready to pass on the wisdom that was so hard won.

The most common place to find a mentor character is in fantasy novels, from Kelsier in *Mistborn* by Brian Sanderson, to Father Chains in *The Lies of Locke Lamora* by Scott Lynch, to Chiron in *The Lightning Thief* by Rick Riordan. The wizard Gandalf is Frodo's mentor in *The Lord of the Rings*. He guides Frodo and his companions on their quest to destroy the ring of power, and travels with them part of the way.

You can find mentors in other genres too. *To All the Boys I've Loved Before* by Jenny Han is a young adult romance about a teenager named Lara Jean, who is the middle of three sisters. Her older sister Margot is her mentor. Their mother is dead, so Margot is practically a parent to her younger sisters. When Margot decides to go abroad for college, she tries to prepare Lara Jean in every way she can, teaching her how to cook, drive carpool, and manage the family schedule.

Like all good mentors, Margot leaves. This is a necessary step to force the heroine to finish growing up on her own. In every book with a mentor, the mentor either leaves or dies. In *To All the Boys I've Loved Before*, the family has been preparing for months for Margot to go to college, but Lara Jean is still startled by it, as if she can't quite believe her sister is leaving. Even at the last minute, she's asking her sister how to make coffee. In *The Lord of the Rings*, Gandalf dies while saving Frodo and his companions from a monster. With Gandalf gone, the fellowship fractures, and Frodo has to make the next move on his own.

If your novel has a mentor character, time the mentor's departure for maximum impact on the protagonist. It should always happen before the hero feels ready for it. In the end, the hero will be fine, and the lessons his mentor taught him will be enough to achieve victory, but in the moment, the loss of his mentor should feel like a huge setback.

The Love Interest

Love interests are important for the plot, and they should influence the story outcome, but their most vital role is thematic. They often represent the internal stakes, whether that's trust, belonging, duty, or self-esteem.

The love interest is better than the protagonist in almost every way. He or she is a companion on the story journey, but the protagonist only becomes worthy of the love interest after they've leveled-up to their full potential.

It's important to understand the difference between a love interest and a romantic partner. As we discussed in chapter three, romantic partners are both co-protagonists and antagonists, causing the other romantic partner to change for the better. However, the love interest doesn't change much, nor does she directly change the heroine. The love interest is the prize that the heroine gains for doing the hard work of changing herself, but the love interest doesn't *force* that change. Romantic partners are only found in romance novels and buddy comedies, but love interests can be found in every genre.

In *The Seven Husbands of Evelyn Hugo* by Taylor Jenkins Reid, Evelyn's one goal is to be famous. She loves fame more than she loves acting. She also loves fame more than she loves her girlfriend. Evelyn and Celia get together, break up, get married to men, get divorced, get together again, and finally settle into happiness together only after Evelyn retires. It takes Evelyn a lifetime to realize that fame is nothing compared to true love. Celia knows this all along, but she doesn't teach this to Evelyn. This is something Evelyn has to learn the hard way.

Mexican Gothic by Silvia Moreno-Garcia is a horror novel that takes place in Mexico in 1950. A graduate student named Noemi has traveled to a remote mountain town to check up on her newlywed cousin, who has been ill. The cousin's house is creepy and weird, and the only person who seems to like Noemi is the caretaker's son. When Noemi discovers that her cousin has married into a family of immortal Nazis, she has to find a way to get her cousin out of there. Her love interest helps her as much as he can, but this is Noemi's fight. The theme of *Mexican Gothic* is a woman's awareness of the world, moving from naivety to wisdom, and Noemi completes this journey on her own. After she burns down her cousin's house and all the evil in it, she and her new love share their first kiss.

If your story has romantic elements, be careful not to fall into stereotypes of the opposite sex, and always give your love interest things to do beyond being the boyfriend or the girlfriend. Because love interests are the prize at the end of the story journey, it's tempting to make them perfect, but it's far better to make them well-rounded characters in their own right. You can even combine them with the believer or doubter character, letting them do double duty and making your story richer.

Family

It's realistic to give your heroine a family, especially in a young adult book where the heroine lives with her parents, or when your book takes place in a small town, where families usually stay close. However, your protagonist's family members still need specific purposes in your story.

It's very common in YA novels for one or both parents to be antagonists. Young adult novels are all about a heroine finding her place in the adult world, and chafing against the older generation is a big part of that. Many grandparents are mentors or believers.

Siblings often show the heroine—and the reader—what she could have been if circumstances were different or if she made different choices. In *Fourth Wing* by Rebecca Yarros, the heroine, Violet, has an older sister named Mira. Unlike Violet, who is physically weaker than her classmates due to a disability, Mira is strong and has been flying dragons into combat for years. Mira is also brash and argumentative, but Violet can't afford to be in conflict with her peers. She must get ahead by forging alliances. If Violet weren't disabled, she might have grown up exactly like Mira. Violet's sister is a funhouse mirror, reflecting what her life could have been, and showing the reader why Violet must choose a different path.

Family is played for laughs in the Stephanie Plum series, from her mother constantly trying to fix Stephanie up with unsuitable men, to her grand-mother disrupting yet another funeral. Their purpose in the novels is to represent the values of their tight-knit Trenton suburb, and to remind Stephanie of all the ways she's not conforming to them.

In *The Stranger* by Harlan Coben, the protagonist, Adam Price, has two teenage sons. When his wife goes missing, the boys miss their mother, and start relying on Price for the things she used to provide, from rides to sports practice to comfort in their distress. But Price, who is frantically looking for his wife, is in no shape to give his sons what they need. As far as the plot goes, the characters of the sons are obstacles, making Price's life harder.

A Balanced Cast

Every character needs a purpose on the page. Your goal is a well-rounded, balanced cast. If you have a character you love who doesn't serve a purpose, you can revise your novel to give her one. Is the quirky aunt kind of like a mentor? Lean into that by giving her more mentor-like attributes. Let her dispense wise advice and set a good example. Has the hero's brother made mistake after mistake in his life? Why not make him a full-blown cautionary tale? Is the heroine's best friend totally on her side, but with some reservations? She can become a useful doubter character if you play up those traits.

Give every character a reason to be in the story. Think about the ways a believer and a doubter echo the voices inside the hero—one pushing him on and one holding him back. Think about when to eliminate the mentor for maximum emotional impact. Think about the ways a cautionary tale can enrich the themes of your novel.

When you're revising, it's not always about addition. Sometimes it's about subtraction. Take an objective look at each character to see if they belong in the novel. Does your heroine need three best friends? Five siblings? Three annoying co-workers? When you start to think of characters in terms of their purpose, you'll find that you don't need as many as you thought. Cut or combine characters when you can. Perhaps instead of three best friends who are all believers, your heroine only needs one.

Eliminate characters, combine their functions, and give all of them a purpose. Get down to the fewest characters your book could possibly have. That's when you know you have the right number.

A Second Look

1. Who is your protagonist's believer? Point to three places in your manuscript where this person shows their belief in the hero. If they aren't on the page, brainstorm ways the believer character can show that they are one hundred percent behind the hero. Mark the places in your manuscript where this will go.

2. Who is your protagonist's doubter? Point to three places in your manuscript where this person cautions the hero not to do things, or do them another way. If they aren't on the page, brainstorm ways the doubter character will try to keep the hero safe. Mark the places in your manuscript where this will go.

3. Does your novel have a cautionary tale? Point to places in your manuscript where you've shown how the heroine could easily end up like him. If they aren't on the page, brainstorm ways to show parallels between the heroine and the cautionary tale. Mark the places in your manuscript where this will go.

4. Does your novel have a mentor character? Open to the place where the mentor leaves or dies. Now move forward in your manuscript

and point to the place where the hero levels up because the mentor is gone. If it's not on the page, brainstorm ways to show the hero taking matters into his own hands, without the safety net of the mentor's presence. Mark the places in your manuscript where this will go.

5. Make a list of every character in your novel and the role each character plays. Look for places to combine roles and eliminate characters, until your novel has the fewest possible characters it could have while still telling the story you want to tell.

NINE

Make a Scene

_____

Each scene in your novel is a building block. Some scenes are cornerstones—the hook, the first plot point, the midpoint, the all-is-lost, and the climax. But there are other, smaller blocks that fill in around them.

Every scene in your book needs essential ingredients like conflict, emotion, and choice, but more than anything else, each scene needs a purpose. What is the point of this scene? Why is it in your novel? Does the heroine learn new information? Is there new danger that raises the stakes? Are you creating romantic tension? Revealing the antagonist's backstory? Does the heroine start to reconsider her life choices? There are countless reasons for a scene to be in your book, but each scene should have more than one reason to be there. Every scene needs to do double duty, both furthering the plot and deepening the character. It's not just about what happens in a scene. There should be an emotional arc for the characters as well.

For example, you might have a scene with a hero—we'll call him Oscar—at a party where he ends up in a swimming pool while fully clothed. He could have fallen in while drunk. He could have been pushed by his rival. He could have decided to jump. These three options spin the plot in three directions. The *why* is important here. Why is Oscar falling-down drunk? Or, why does someone hate him enough to push him into a swimming pool? Or, what is his reason for jumping in? Oscar's emotions around the dunking are also revealing. Is he mortified? Angry? Does he think it's funny? How a character reacts to events tells the reader who they are.

An action scene without thought and emotion will feel flat. Add character to your action scenes. But just as bad is a one-note scene that exists only to reveal character. Look for scenes that are pure character scenes and see if you can combine them with a scene that has some action in it. Readers want to learn who the hero is while we watch him trying to solve his problems.

Active Scenes

Every scene begins with a problem. It can be an obvious problem like an incoming threat or someone actively stopping the heroine on her quest. It can also be a more subtle problem like an unfulfilled desire or an unanswered question. If your scene isn't about trying to solve an immediate problem, you should revise or cut that scene.

There shouldn't be any scenes in your book that are meant to set up the situation or tell the reader the backstory. You have to provide background, of course, but the best place to insert explanation is within the context of the current problem. Always be thinking about forward movement.

A scene runs on conflict. The hero must be in direct confrontation with someone else. Internal conflict is important too, but even if there's internal conflict, each scene must have external conflict as well. In fact, the internal conflict should be revealed by the external conflict.

Let's say your heroine's mother is in the hospital, in intensive care. You could write a static scene of the heroine sitting at her mother's bedside, thinking about her relationship with her mother, feeling guilt that she was never there when her mom needed her. Lots of thinking. Lots of feeling. But no doing. This is the place where the reader puts the book down and turns on the TV.

A better choice would be to make the conflict external. Visiting hours are over, but the heroine refuses to leave her mother's side. She gets into an argument with the nurse who tries to kick her out. The heroine knows she should leave, but she feels overwhelmingly guilty. She yells at the nurse, saying that she wasn't there for her mother when she should have been but by God, she's going to be here now. The *external* conflict with the nurse is the hook that you hang the *internal* conflict on. Putting them together makes for a rounded scene.

Readers don't believe anything unless you show it to them in the form of character action. Heroes are only human, and humans change their minds a hundred times a day. You can have an idea and then immediately talk yourself out of it. You might think, "I should make that phone call," or "I should ask for a raise," or "I should tell my crush how I feel about him," but you never do it. This is why it's always a bad idea to have your hero sitting in a room thinking thoughts. Once a character takes action, then we know that it's for real.

It's not enough for each scene to have a goal. There has to be the flip side of that goal. Something bad will happen to your hero if he fails. Let's say your hero is a stamp collector and he's trying to buy a rare stamp from a dealer who doesn't want to sell it for a fair price. Your hero has a problem: he needs the stamp. He's proactive: he's trying to buy it from the dealer. There is conflict: the dealer won't come down in price. But it's missing the consequences for failure. After all, the hero can meet the seller's price. Or he can try other stamp dealers. Or he can just not buy the stamp today. You can write a scene with a proactive hero working toward his goal. You can write that scene with conflict. But if you neglect consequences, the reader won't care.

How could you add consequences for failure to this scene? Let's say the stamp is the only one of its kind. Let's also say your hero has already pre-arranged to resell it for a higher price. And in order to buy the stamp in the first place he got a loan from a loan shark who is going to break his legs if he's not repaid. The interest payments are already adding up. Now we've got consequences for failure. Now your hero *must* buy the stamp at a good price. Now we've got a reason for your reader to keep turning the pages.

Scenes should end in disaster. The problem isn't solved, or the problem gets worse, or the problem *does* get solved in a way that leads to further complications. But whatever happens, your hero should not be in the same circumstances he was at the beginning of the scene. The plot has moved forward, and he's in a different frame of mind or has new emotions.

In *The Seven Husbands of Evelyn Hugo*, Evelyn describes her second marriage to a Hollywood legend. She goes into great detail about how blissfully happy they were, how their wedding was like a fairy tale, and how in love with him she was. The chapter ends with the revelation that six months into their marriage, her husband began beating her. This devastating reversal makes for a powerful scene.

Go back to that quick outline you wrote. Look at

each individual scene and mark the change that occurs. If you find a static scene, you can either cut it, combine it with another scene, or revise it to add complications and new consequences.

Reaction Scenes

Novels aren't all relentless forward motion. Even in the most fast-paced thriller, characters need time to regroup and choose their next course of action. There should be moments between the action beats where your heroine feels, thinks, and decides.

These reaction scenes are especially important right after the big turning point scenes, when your protagonist has just been through a major upheaval. She's been hurled into a new life at plot point one, or she's had a huge revelation at the midpoint that's upended everything. Or she's bottomed out at the all-is-lost moment. She should be having lots of emotions about these events. But these aren't the only places to add reaction scenes. Every big action should be followed by an equally big reaction. Be careful that you're not racing to the next plot event without letting your heroine process what just happened to her.

Let's go back to Oscar, who went into the swimming pool fully clothed. You'd expect some reaction to that. How does he feel about it? Is he humiliated? Does he try to brush it off, staying cool, while dying a little inside? Is he fuming with hatred for the person who pushed him in? Does he laugh and treat it like a great joke? The reaction beat starts with Oscar's emotions.

After the emotion comes the thought. Does Oscar think about what an idiot move that was? Does he immediately start plotting revenge? Does he wonder how he's going to dry off, since he's at his girlfriend's house with no clean clothes?

Next comes the decision. What is he going to do about this? Tackle his rival and throw him into the pool? Ask his girlfriend for help? Try to make a distraction so he can sneak away unnoticed?

It's important that you have all three components —emotion, thought, decision—and that you put them in this order. The emotional response and the thought process tells you a lot about who this character is. The decision should lead the hero directly into the next action scene.

Note that these reaction beats slow the story down temporarily, but that doesn't mean your hero has stopped moving forward. He should be actively deciding what to do next. His thoughts and feelings are pushing him to make that decision, and it shouldn't take long for your hero to figure out his next steps.

Things to avoid here are a hero feeling sorry for himself and a hero feeling hopeless. Protagonists should have agency and they should be proactive. Even when it looks bleak, they'll keep trying.

Be careful about how much time you're allocating to these reaction beats. Too much will slow your book to a crawl. However, too little is just as bad. Without emotion and thought, your characters will be as two-dimensional as a character in a video game, moving through the stages of the plot simply because that's what comes next.

Genre plays a big part in how much page time is devoted to action and how much to reaction. In genres such as thriller and action-adventure stories, the pace is so fast that the hero is moving from disaster to disaster with hardly any time to feel or think. This is what readers expect and want from that kind of novel. The reaction is usually built into the active scene itself and the decision is made without much thought because the next course of action is obvious. After all, if the villain has bombed the hero's house, there's not much he can do except run away from the explosion. He'll have his emotions and thoughts *while* he's running away, and by the time he gets to safety, he's already decided what to do next.

However, other genres require longer reaction scenes. Protagonists in romance, literary fiction, horror, and most young adult books need time to process their emotions and think things over before moving to more action. Don't rush the reaction beats in these genres. If you do, your characters will seem underdeveloped and the events of your plot will seem random, rather than purposeful.

This is another place where your quick outline comes in handy. You can use it to mark the action and reaction beats in your story. If you see that you have four action scenes in a row, with nobody able to catch their breath, you'll want to break it up with a reaction scene or two. If you've got your hero thinking and feeling for several scenes in a row, it's time to get him up and moving into a new decision that leads to action.

How to Start a Scene

Every time you start a new scene, you have to hook your reader all over again, so you're constantly giving the reader a reason to keep reading. Not every scene has to start with a bang, but every scene needs to start with something that's going to interest the reader and get her invested for one more page or one more chapter.

Examine the start of each of your scenes. You can start with action, summary, thought, setting, or dialogue. No matter how you start a scene, you must orient the reader right away. Help the reader understand who the point of view character is, and how much time has passed since the last scene. It can be as simple as "Three days later, Charlie was surprised to see Fatima at the library." Or, "As soon as she got home from work, Nora checked on the kittens."

You can start a scene with action, without stopping for explanation, setting, or motivation. Readers don't mind starting a scene this way if something interesting is happening on the page, even if they don't quite understand it yet. Lots of thrillers start each scene with a hero running, hiding, or evading. If you're using this technique, you'll have to explain as you go, or put in some explanation immediately after the action is complete. Be careful that you don't lose your reader.

You can start a scene with summary. This is useful for big transitions, when your last scene ended in one place or time and your next scene opens somewhere else. How did you get there? How much time has passed? You can do a quick summary to orient your reader and then move into the action.

You might start your scene like this: "Clara drove to her sister's house in a panic. When she arrived, Irene was waiting on the porch, clutching her cell phone and crying." In this example, you're giving the reader a summary of what happened between the last scene and this one, so she has all the information she needs to begin the main action of this scene.

You can begin a scene with thought. In *The Martian*, many chapters begin with Watney contemplating how large Mars is and how alone he is there. But when you start a scene with thinking, make sure you don't *continue* with thinking for too long. Your hero can ponder ideas, especially while deciding what to do, but shouldn't get lost in thought. Pretty soon, within a paragraph or two, he should be up and moving.

If you're starting a scene with setting, don't start with static description. Start with your hero interacting with the setting. He shouldn't be standing still, staring at the mountain in front of him. He should be climbing that mountain. You can describe the rocks as he steps on them, the tree roots as he trips over them, and the stream as he wades through it. This is how you should be handling description all the time, but especially at the beginning of a scene.

You can start with dialogue, but this is a technique to use sparingly. Readers don't mind jumping into action right away, but they have a harder time jumping into dialogue right away. Did you ever sit on a park bench, or in the waiting room of a doctor's office, and have someone sit down right next to you and start talking on their cell phone? Annoying, isn't it? Overhearing that disembodied conversation, with no context, grates on the nerves. That's how readers feel when they're asked to jump into a section of dialogue with no grounding.

But it *can* work. If you want to see an example done well, read *Tempting Taste* by Sara Whitney. Nearly every scene begins with dialogue. We're thrown directly into the hero or heroine's point of view, and the conflict has already begun. She might start with a bestie trying to get a look at scandalous pictures on the heroine's phone, or the heroine arriving at the hero's door early in the morning and demanding he get dressed and go with her, or a friend complaining about a bad haircut. But Whitney doesn't just give us floating heads. Each scene is grounded in time and place. The dialogue is snappy, and it's a quick start to a scene. It's appropriate for a romantic comedy with off-the-charts banter.

Opening a scene with dialogue is tricky. I'd recommend other ways to start a scene, and only use dialogue if nothing else works. If you decide to begin with conversation, ground readers in time and place as soon as possible.

How to End a Scene

The last sentence in each scene must prompt the reader to continue on to the next. It can be as big as a massive cliffhanger or as subtle as an unanswered question, but whatever it is, you must give your reader a reason to turn the page. You can end scenes with emotional turmoil, new information, an epiphany, a promise, or a cliffhanger.

Emotional turmoil is a good way to end a scene that comes right after some huge action, turning point, or revelation. You've had the main action of the scene, ending with an emotional blow. The heroine is still dealing with those feelings when the chapter ends. This is ideal for romance, young adult fiction, or literary fiction, but it can be used in all genres.

You can end a scene with new information. This is a time-honored way to end scenes in crime fiction. The PI talks to a witness, learns valuable information that changes the direction of the case, and that's the end of the scene. However, this can also be used in other genres, such as the discovery of a family secret, or news that your hero's mother-in-law is going to stay for a month, or that your heroine is pregnant. The reader will keep reading to find out the consequences of this information.

An epiphany is often used to end scenes in literary fiction, women's fiction, young adult fiction, or romance. If you're ending the scene with an epiphany, the hero or heroine has a huge revelation that things weren't the way they seemed. It can be as big as "You're working for *them* aren't you?" or as small as, "Wow, my sister has a good side I never knew existed." Whatever it is, the reader is aware that this new understanding will lead the plot in a new direction, and she'll read on to find out what that direction is.

You can also end with a promise of things to come. Leave something hanging, something the readers know will happen, but they have to keep reading to see it. One character says, "Meet me at Lefty's Bar at eleven o'clock and I'll tell you what you want to know." Or, "Tomorrow when I go into work, I'm going to show my boss what I really think of her." Or the playground bully telling the little kid, "Just wait until recess, then you're going to get it." The reader will read on to see if everything will work out or not.

The queen of all scene endings is the cliffhanger, which is when you end a scene just before the action resolves. This is great right after a huge plot twist, or after a big reversal of fortune for your protagonist.

Remember, if you do this, you can't skip the reaction scene. You'll have to put all the emotional fallout from this event into the beginning of the next chapter. If you want to see great examples of cliffhangers, read *The DaVinci Code* by Dan Brown. Every single chapter ended on a cliffhanger. When I was reading that book, I always stopped in the middle of a chapter, because I knew if I read to the end of the chapter, I'd start the next one.

A Second Look

1. Open the outline you made of your novel at the beginning of your revision process. Write down the purpose of each scene. Look for both outer conflict and inner turmoil. If a scene has only one purpose, or it duplicates the purpose of another scene, brainstorm ways to eliminate or combine scenes, and make detailed notes about what you'll change and exactly where those changes will go in the manuscript.

2. Write down the change that occurs as a result of each scene. Note both how circumstances are different at the end of the scene than they were at the beginning, and how the protagonist has changed. If you find a scene with no change, then it's not furthering the story and should be cut, combined with another scene, or revised to add consequences.

3. Mark each scene in your outline as either an action scene or a reaction scene. Look for a back-and-forth pattern of action and reaction. If you notice that you have too many of one kind of scene in a row, rearrange things, combine scenes, or cut scenes to bring your story back into rhythm.

4. Open your manuscript and look at the beginning of each scene. Write down the exact way you've hooked readers. Look at the end of each scene. Write down the exact way you've prompted them to keep reading. If you aren't constantly pulling readers through the story, revise the opening and closing of scenes to add impact.

TEN

Dialogue

_____

Characters must talk to each other, but dialogue on the page is nothing like dialogue in real life. Real-life dialogue is full of filler words and small talk, meant to pass the time and bond friendships. But fictional dialogue has more important jobs to do. It has to fuel conflict and deepen characterization, all while sounding natural on the page. Fictional dialogue is artificial and stylized, but it needs to give the illusion of actual speech.

Every line of dialogue in your story needs to be earned. When your characters speak, it should serve some purpose in the story. When you're revising, take a hard look at each line of dialogue. You should know what the characters want in that particular scene, and what they will say to get it.

In your first draft, it's perfectly okay to write

dialogue that's bland and filled with cliches, with your characters saying exactly what's on their minds. In your first draft, you were concentrating on what you wanted your characters to say. In the second draft, you can figure out how they should say it. Now is your chance to add personality and nuance to every line of dialogue.

Clean Up Your Dialogue

Start by cleaning up your dialogue. Get rid of small talk and expository dialogue, add action and emotion, and tighten sentences whenever you can.

Never allow your characters to engage in idle chitchat without purpose. It stops the story dead in its tracks.

"Hello Becky, how have you been?"

"I'm doing okay, Anna. How are you?"

"Fine, thanks."

"How are David and the kids?"

"They're doing well."

"Good to hear."

"It's nice to see you out on such a beautiful day."

"I know! Can you believe this weather?"

"It sure has been nice lately."

This kind of dialogue will put your reader to sleep. It doesn't move the plot along, nor does it illuminate character. The purpose of dialogue is to communicate what the characters want in a scene. Small talk indicates that they want nothing, and strive for nothing. When you're revising, be on high alert for this kind of placeholder dialogue. You don't have to rewrite it. You can simply remove it.

The flip side of small talk is expository dialogue, where two characters tell each other things they both already know.

"Honey, we should visit your sister in California in September."

"My sister has three kids, and you've seen how small her house is. There wouldn't be room for us."

This kind of dialogue is unnatural and annoying to read. Both characters in this scene know that the sister lives in California. They both know she has three kids. They both know her house is small. However, the author wants the reader to know this information, so it's crammed into dialogue, where it doesn't belong.

You also hear this kind of dialogue in action movies, where one character will shout a super obvious warning to the other characters, even though everyone in this scene knows about the danger ahead.

"If we don't disarm this bomb in the next five

minutes, the whole warehouse will blow up and kill us both!"

Action movies can get away with this. Novels can't. Avoid dialogue that only exists to tell the reader information, especially obvious information. It's okay for one character to inform another about something that they don't know, but it's not okay to tell the reader something that everyone on the page already knows. Characters should only talk to one another, not to the reader.

This includes one character calling another by name. On TV, characters call each other by name all the time. This is for the benefit of the viewer. How else would the casual viewer who doesn't tune in every single week know that Lady Crawford's name is Lady Crawford? So you get dialogue like this:

> "Welcome, Lady Crawford. We're so glad you could join us."
>
> "I simply couldn't stay away, Lydia. Is your sister at home?"
>
> "Mary will be joining us presently, Lady Crawford."

Real people don't routinely call each other by name in casual conversation. We call someone by name when we need to get his attention, as in, "Dad, look!" Or as an expression of surprise. "Omar! I'm so glad you could make it." A name sometimes comes in the middle of an argument, but keep in mind that this feels extremely hostile. "This ends now, Jake. Leave me alone or I'm calling the cops."

Outside of those rare instances, you don't need to have one character use another's name. It's already in the narration, so the reader already knows it.

Rhythm and Emotion

The second draft is the ideal time to add rhythm and emotion to your dialogue by adding action beats. Let's say your scene takes place at a theme park, where your twelve-year-old protagonist has just stepped off the biggest, baddest roller coaster. Her dialogue might go like this:

> "I can't believe I rode The Raptor. I mean, look at that thing. Could you ever imagine me up there? Me? When that coaster kept climbing, I thought I was going to puke, and that first hill almost killed me. I could have been a goner. *Whoosh.* That was some ride."

This passage feels realistic, with the punchy speech rhythms of a tween, but it's fairly dense on the page, and the reader has the sense of being talked at. There's also a bit of disconnect, because it's not clear from the dialogue alone if the speaker is terrified or proud. You can help the reader by incorporating action between beats of dialogue.

Here's our tween feeling nauseated and still shaky.

"I can't believe I rode The Raptor. I mean, look at that thing. Could you ever imagine me up there? Me?" Claire put a hand to her heart and plopped down on a bench, her face pale. "When that coaster kept climbing, I thought I was going to puke, and that first hill almost killed me. I could have been a goner." She put her head between her knees. "*Whoosh*. That was some ride."

Here's our same character, with the same dialogue, only now she's thrilled and proud of herself.

"I can't believe I rode The Raptor. I mean, look at that thing. Could you ever imagine me up there? Me?" Claire tilted her head back and giggled. She snatched a handful of her sister's popcorn and shoved it into her mouth. "When that coaster kept climbing, I thought I was going to puke, and that first hill almost killed me. I could have been a goner." She spun in a circle and then danced back to her family. "*Whoosh*. That was some ride."

The author could have broken up the wall of dialogue by having Claire walking with her family to the next coaster, or putting on more sunscreen, or retying her shoe, or stepping over a puddle, but that would have been a wasted opportunity. By showing Claire trying not to vomit or dancing in a circle, the author is showing the reader what the heroine's mental state is, without having to spell it out. Readers would much rather figure this out for themselves by the clues you leave them.

With each pass through the manuscript, look at places to tighten your dialogue. Do you need five back-and-forth exchanges, or will one punchy sentence do? Can your characters get to the point faster, or in a more succinct way?

Maybe one of your characters has doubts about their next course of action. You could have her say, "Well, I don't know. Are we sure we want to do that? Seems risky. It might not work."

The problem? She's basically saying the same thing four times. You need to look at your character's personality, to see which expression suits her best.

Is she indecisive? She might say, "Well, I don't know…"

Is she timid? She might say, "Are we sure we want to do that?"

Is she forthright? She might say, "No. Too risky."

Is she pessimistic? She might say, "It might not work."

You might think you need all those sentences, but less is more here. If you have all of them, your message gets muddled and you don't have a clear sense of who your character is. So pick one, maybe two, but don't pick all four.

Explaining Experience, Hiding Emotion

Your second draft is your chance to turn generic, bland dialogue into dialogue that's specific and unusual. Look for places to add sparkle by adding concrete details.

A mom shouldn't tell her son that his room is too messy. She should say, "I'm wading through laundry up to my ankles."

Instead of asking, "Are you eating enough?" your character should say, "Have you eaten anything besides an orange today?"

Instead of accusing her friend of being a workaholic, your character should say, "When's the last time you took a vacation? 2009?"

These characters are not being poetic. They're not using fancy language. They aren't even exaggerating. They're saying exactly what they mean by using specific language that speaks to their immediate experience.

However, characters do *not* say what they mean when it comes to their internal state. Humans rarely talk directly about emotions. It's awkward. It's embarrassing. There's too much to lose. When dialogue is simply one character telling another about their emotional state, it's known as *on-the-nose* dialogue.

Readers hate it. On-the-nose dialogue makes them feel talked down to, and, ironically, it makes the character seem less trustworthy, since humans simply don't talk like this.

There's one exception to this, which we'll discuss below, but for the most part, people don't go around explaining their emotions to one another, and your characters shouldn't do it either.

When it comes to our true feelings, we hide our emotions in sarcasm, misdirection, or understatement. When you're revising, trust your reader to understand the meaning from more subtle clues. And trust yourself to get the information across without characters functioning as amateur therapists for one another.

An older man might invite his children and grandchildren for Sunday dinner, cook them a roast with all the trimmings, pour the wine, and then lift his glass, look at his big family seated around the table, and say, "I'm glad we're all here." What he means is I love you, and I appreciate you, and I'm grateful that you're saving me from loneliness, but that kind of on-the-nose dialogue isn't realistic in fiction or in life, so he says something like, "I'm glad we're all here."

Or consider a teenage boy getting up the courage to ask a girl he likes to the movies. If she turns him down, he wouldn't say, "Oh gee, now I'm embarrassed and a little hurt. It took me all week to get up the courage to ask you." No teenage boy has ever said those words. Instead, he'd put on a brave face and say something like, "No big deal. I have stuff to do on Saturday night anyway."

Look at your novel's dialogue for places where characters are explaining their feelings to one another, and find ways to make your dialogue more subtle and more realistic.

Metaphor Sets

In most first drafts, all the characters sound the same. They all sound like the author, using the vocabulary and figures of speech that the author herself would use. The result is flat characters who the reader can't tell apart.

Nothing shows characterization more than dialogue. Before you revise the words that come out of a character's mouth, you need to look deeply at the character to know who he is. A character's speech reflects their age, their education level, their social class, their occupation, their values, their interests, and so much more.

A woman with a PhD who lives in Toronto is going to speak much differently than a middle school kid from San Antonio. A man whose hobbies are playing piano and composing classical music is going to speak much differently than a man whose hobbies are axe throwing and attending NASCAR races. A grandmother sounds different than her teenaged grandson.

We touched on this in chapter seven when we

discussed voice in your description, but it becomes even more important in dialogue. The best way to make your characters distinct is to give each character their own unique metaphor set.

Let's make up a character. Let's say she's a twenty-one-year-old cocktail waitress at one of the casinos in Las Vegas. Dad is long gone and our heroine lives with her mom, who works as a maid cleaning rooms at the Bellagio. What kind of expressions would our heroine use? She might say she was dealt a lousy hand in life. If she was committing to something, she'd say she's putting all her chips on the table. If she was feeling lucky, she might say, "It's all aces." These are the kinds of expressions that come easily to her because they reflect her lived experience.

Now let's think of a very different character—a Midwestern mom who lives in the suburbs and loves to garden. She's going to have very different expressions top-of-mind when she speaks. If she's feeling lucky, she won't say, "It's all aces." That would be a weird thing for her to say. Instead, if she's feeling lucky, she might say that she feels "like a kid with an unexpected snow day." She might describe a naive friend as being "very green," or call her new neighbors "transplants from Ohio."

Or maybe your character is a chef from New York. If he was feeling lucky, what would he say? "I feel like I'm sitting at the best table." He'd say his girlfriend is as sweet as caramel, or describe his enemy as a bitter old hag. If he was having a bad day, he might say, "stick a fork in me, I'm done."

Characters say what they know. The expressions they use come directly from their lives. Giving your characters a metaphor set that makes sense for who they are will elevate your dialogue, cement your character in the reader's mind, and make each character unique.

Conflict in Dialogue

Almost every novel has characters who lie. Sometimes the lie is obvious, and sometimes the reader only suspects that this character isn't telling the truth. When someone is truthful, his body language will align with his words. But when someone's lying, his body language will often give away the lie. Is he shuffling uncomfortably from foot to foot? Is he avoiding another character's eyes? Is he wiping nervous sweat from his neck? Look at the actual words of the dialogue as well. Liars say "um" and "er" a lot. They stumble over their words. They'll use the words "believe me," or "in all honesty," and say them with false sincerity.

Deceivers complain a lot, trying to shift blame onto another person, or they give overly complicated answers to simple questions. Here's an example.

Cara didn't meet her mother's eyes. "Honestly, Mom, I didn't go to the bonfire with those boys. They, like, went without me." Her foot jiggled under the table. "You have to believe me. I was home. I loaded the dishwasher, didn't I? And you say I never help out at home. I'm so unappreciated around here. You don't think I can do anything right."

Cara is clearly trying to get her mom to argue with her about helping out at home rather than asking where she was last night.

In a novel, characters will be in conflict more often than they're not, since conflict is what moves a story forward. The conflict might be with weapons or fists, but most of the time, that conflict will be with words. Your hero wants something. Someone else doesn't want them to have it. It can be as small as a kid not wanting to eat his vegetables or as big as a superhero trying to stop the supervillain from destroying the world.

People often begin arguments with the assumption that if the other person would just *understand* their position, they'd agree. Characters will repeat themselves in the beginning of arguments, as they cling ever more tightly to their positions and try to get the other party to see their point of view.

During the middle of an argument, characters won't stop to consider what the other person says. Characters will interrupt each other. Revise your sentences to make them short and choppy, with characters cutting each other off.

When the characters realize that the other person is not going to listen, or even try to understand, that's when it gets personal and vicious. The most powerful word you can use in an argument is the word *you*.

"You never listen."

"You're impossible to deal with."

"I can't believe you said that."

The hottest part of the argument should be all about finger-pointing and accusations. Below is an excerpt from *Tempting Taste* by Sara Whitney. Erik, a shy baker, is dating Josie, an outgoing marketing expert. She pushes him to be interviewed on TV, giving him no choice, and no time to back out of it. He's upset that she's putting her own ambition over his comfort. After the filming, their argument reaches a high point.

Erik turned on his heel and stormed out of the studio. Josie caught up to him in the hallway, where he was leaning against the wall, body rigid.

"Erik, what's—?"

"Next time, ask." His jaw barely moved, and each word pierced her like a knife.

"What do you mean? You were great!"

"I was terrified."

She fell silent, processing his words. "And now you're mad."

"I'm *furious*. Do you think any part of me wanted to do that?"

"Well, n-no. Not at first," she stammered. "But I thought you'd—"

He turned his glittering eyes on her. "Thought I'd do whatever you wanted?"

"When it comes to marketing, yes. You said you trusted me."

"I trusted that you knew me."

"I *do* know you."

He shook his head once, sharply. "Then you should know that I would never want *that*."

Notice how often the word *you* is used here. Both Erik and Josie are telling the other, "you did this," and "you did that."

The hottest part of the argument is also the most honest. This is the point where the character realizes he has nothing to lose anymore, so he might as well tell the truth. We see that in the excerpt from *Tempting Taste*. Erik is extremely honest about how that TV interview made him feel. He was terrified, and he's furious at Josie for making him do it.

Once the character is pushed to that point, he's going all the way. Here, characters say unforgivable things like, "Our family was perfect before you were born." Or, "That car crash was your fault and you know it." Or, "You drove your husband away."

This isn't something to take lightly. A character

can't start by dropping emotional truth bombs right off the bat. This is something he has to be pushed into. The only place this kind of on-the-nose dialogue works is at the white-hot center of an argument. When you're revising, cut that kind of dialogue from everywhere else and put it here.

The relationship between the characters is different after the fight. Things have been said that can't be unsaid. The characters know things about the other person they didn't know before, and they understand each other on a whole new level. If the relationship between characters *doesn't* change after an argument, then there was no point in writing it.

When two characters are in conflict, keep in mind the power dynamics between them. If a teenager has forgotten to wheel the trash bins to the curb three weeks in a row, the argument with his dad is going to look quite different depending on whose point of view you're writing from. Dad has all the power in this scenario, and the teen doesn't have a leg to stand on. Same with a boss and employee, or a law enforcement officer and a suspect.

Social power applies here too. The most popular girl in school can get away with insults that the less popular kids wouldn't dare. In historical fiction, think about a lady arguing with her maid. The maid has to bring up her concerns very gently, very lightly, and very indirectly, whereas the lady can say whatever she wants.

You can't have a good argument without good insults, and the best insults are personal. If your character wants to insult someone, don't rely on something generic like saying he's ugly or he's stupid. That's not good enough. An insult should be crafted to take a shot at whatever the character is the most insecure about.

Is your teenage heroine struggling with acne, and unsuccessful at finding treatment or coverups? Have the mean girl stand next to her at the school's bathroom sink and give her false sympathy. "It must be such a burden to have constant breakouts. I don't know what I would do if I had skin like yours." That's the kind of insult that's going to hurt your heroine deeply.

Or perhaps a suburbanite has been working hard all summer to get his lawn in shape after dealing with a grub infestation, and he's finally got a few green patches to grow, giving him hope. The evil neighbor could tell him, "It's too bad nothing seems to take in your yard. It seems like no matter what you do, you can't get grass to grow there." When you're revising your dialogue, make sure your insults stab right to the heart.

Should you use profanity in your novel? That depends on the genre and audience. Some genres use a lot, some almost none. Pay attention to the norms for your novel's category. If you're writing a fantasy novel, and you're inventing new swear words for your fantasy world, keep in mind that swear words usually involve body parts, or taking the name of a god in vain. And if you can combine them, it will help your invented curse words seem like real curse words. If you're using something like *Odin's butthole,* you're probably on the right track.

Specialized Dialogue

There comes a point in nearly every story where you'll have to explain some insider knowledge and vocabulary. If your story takes place in a courtroom, you need to explain a few things to the reader. What is the difference between manslaughter and murder? What's a bench warrant? Why do grand juries meet in secret? This type of story uses words that the average reader isn't familiar with.

If your hero makes artisan soap, he's going to use words like emulsion, trace, and gel phase. If your hero is a composer, he's going to need staff paper, or he'll use Finale on his computer. The key to dialogue that includes jargon is to find subtle ways to explain what it means without interrupting the flow. You can do this with context clues, internal thoughts, or by having a seasoned pro explain the jargon to a newbie. Be careful with this last one. It's all too easy to slip into expositional dialogue. Find other ways to clue the reader in if you can.

Slang is another kind of insider speech, but in this case, it's social and cultural rather than industry-specific. The problem with slang is how quickly it changes. For example, what if you're talking about something that is good, fashionable, or the latest must-have item? It might be the bee's knees, the cat's pajamas, swell, hip, groovy, far out, awesome, killer, rad, sick, da bomb, phat, lit, or sick. These are all ways your character could communicate that they approve of and admire something, and all are associated with certain time periods or certain groups. A modern teenager wouldn't call something groovy or hip, while very few grandmothers describe things as "da bomb." Slang is an ever-changing aspect of culture, so it's always going to date a story.

Sometimes that can work to your advantage. In historical fiction, it can help establish the time period. Fantasy and science fiction can sometimes benefit from invented slang. But for most contemporary fiction, slang should be used sparingly and intentionally.

Dialect is another minefield. It can add a sense of authenticity to a story, and it can enrich the setting, particularly if the story revolves around a culture that uses a variant of standard English. Some good examples of dialect usage in dialogue are *House of Cotton* by Monica Brashears, *Where the Crawdads Sing* by Delia Owens, and *Kindred* by Octavia Butler.

However, unless you're from the culture you're portraying, or you've done an ungodly amount of research, you shouldn't try to write in dialect. Appropriating a culture not your own is offensive, and trying to write a dialect you're not intimately familiar with rarely ends well. There are thousands of ways to tell every story. Try to find one that sidesteps this particular minefield.

Writing dialogue for kids is another challenge. Many writers either make their tots too wise or make older kids sound like babies. You need to understand child development to understand their worldview. Kids think in terms of school years, not calendar years. Their milestones are learning to ride a bike, getting their first phone, learning to drive, and having their first kiss. They don't take the long view or see the bigger picture. Nor do they get nostalgic. Whatever is in front of them is the most important thing, and they're constantly comparing themselves to their peers to see where they fit.

Dialogue in kid lit is usually shorter. Kids do a lot of back and forth, with a lot of interruptions, and their dialogue is more concrete than abstract. Dialogue communicates what the characters want in the scene. What kids want is different than what adults want. Keep that in mind when polishing dialogue for young characters.

Historical fiction comes with its own set of challenges. You have to work hard to ground the reader in the story world, and dialogue is a big part of that. If you're not careful, you can burst the bubble, pulling readers out of the story. You need to give the illusion of dialogue that would be spoken in the time period, while making it understandable to the modern reader. Dialogue in historical fiction is often sanitized, especially in historical romance, leaving out the sexist, racist, and ableist language that was common in the past. It's a delicate balancing act to leave in enough authentic language to reflect the flavor of the past while keeping the dialogue pleasing to the modern reader.

If you write historical fiction, you should read lots of books in your genre, read fiction from the time period your book is set in, and read original sources like diaries and letters. Then, read your dialogue out loud to see how it sounds to a modern ear.

Banter

Flirting is playful, full of rhythm and wordplay. Readers love it when dialogue is witty and fast-paced, and they adore a good zinger. In order for banter to work well, one character must notice and comment on the other's appearance, behavior, or habits. It flatters the receiver and shows that the giver was paying attention.

Banter needs to be light, not mean-spirited. Instead of teasing someone about their insecurities, banter often goes after what someone is proud of. For example, a studious character who gets high marks in school might be called "the brains around here."

Someone with luscious long hair might be told that she looks like a Disney princess.

Banter is play. Two characters are playing a game together using words, so quick thinking and wit matter a lot. One character will deliberately mistake the other's meaning, or reverse their statement, or stretch it to an illogical conclusion, as in the following example.

> "I used to think you're full of yourself." Patrick leaned in closer. "But clearly you've made room for me."
>
> Shayla's mouth quirked up. "Careful, or I might start charging you rent."

While engaging in flirty banter, the body language of both characters needs to indicate that this is all in good fun. There should be smiles, nods, and leaning in. Closed-off body language such as crossed arms shows that the banter has gone too far, and has degraded into bickering.

Banter is all about relationships. It's one party testing the boundaries of another, or purposely pushing buttons to see how far they can go. Banter is always filled with subtext, which is what makes it so fun to read. The characters are telling each other how they feel without telling each other how they feel. The following example might be a bit more obvious than we'd like, but it shows what makes banter work.

Sam stepped into Hotshot Coffee, tucking his newest book under his arm. Lila was already waiting, leaning on the register with a smirk that spelled trouble.

"Let me guess," she said. "Black coffee and a scone. Again. Living life dangerously, I see."

"I like to keep you on your toes."

"Every day, I think, *Maybe today's the day he orders something different.*" Lila shook her head with mock despair. "Maybe even a latte. With flavor. Keeps me up at night."

"I'll try not to disrupt your sleep schedule." Sam handed over a five-dollar bill, then slid another into the tip jar, trying not to think about Lila lying awake, wondering about him.

She grinned as she rang him up. "You're predictable. It's comforting."

"I'll let you know if I ever snap and order a croissant. Might need you to talk me through it."

"I'll bring a paper bag for the hyperventilating." She handed over his coffee and scone, her grin widening as she caught sight of the book under his arm. She tapped the corner. "*The History of Bookbinding Techniques.* Sounds riveting."

He lowered his voice and leaned in. "Daring escapades in the librarian world."

"No wonder you keep your breakfast boring," she said. "Your life is already filled with so much excitement."

"I never know what you're going to say next, so this daily conversation is about all the excitement I can take."

Lila played with the collar of her shirt, then ran a hand down her side. "Sometimes you need to be brave. You know, take a risk."

It's clear that Lila and Sam enjoy each other's company, each of them lingering over what could be a straightforward transaction. Their body language shows interest, in the way they smile at each other and lean in. Lila touches Sam's book since she can't touch him. Their dialogue shows how much they pay attention to the other. Lila teases Sam about his predictability. Sam notes Lila's spontaneity. Lila wants Sam to ask her out, and is giving him all the hints in the world to nudge him in that direction.

It only takes a few quick lines to establish a connection through banter. Letting it go on too long robs the conversation of its focus and you'll lose the subtext. It's fun to write zinging one-liners and play with quotable dialogue, but don't let the fun stuff take away from the real purpose of dialogue, which is to keep the story moving forward.

Read it Aloud

When revising, the final test of your dialogue is always to read it out loud. If you stumble anywhere, or have a hard time getting the words out, try rewriting the passage. Watch for places where you need to catch your breath because a sentence has gone on too long. Notice where you're rearranging words to sound better. Check your body language as you read, and see where you've grimaced at an awkward phrase or slumped in your chair out of boredom. You might think that these things don't matter because the dialogue is on the page, not spoken aloud, but readers "hear" the dialogue as they read it, and they'll notice when it doesn't flow. Make your dialogue smooth to both the eye and the ear.

A Second Look

1. Read through your manuscript's dialogue. Clean it up by getting rid of small talk, expository dialogue, or generic dialogue. Replace it with dialogue that is specific, reflecting the characters' experiences. Keep in mind the purpose of dialogue, which is to deepen characterization and fuel conflict.

2. Revisit the first exercise in chapter seven where you wrote down six qualities that define your protagonist. Use those qualities to give her a unique metaphor set. Use that metaphor set for her dialogue.

3. Now write down six qualities that define the antagonist. Use those qualities to give him a unique metaphor set. Use that metaphor set for his dialogue.

4. Do the same thing for the minor characters.

5. Examine the arguments in your novel. Let them build from one character trying to convince another, to more strident sentences, to making it personal, to the white-hot center where accusations fly and characters are finally

honest. If your arguments don't progress like this, rewrite them in a more focused way.

6. For each argument in your novel, write down how your characters and their situation are changed after the fight. If things haven't changed after the argument, then cut it or revise it to make the argument affect the outcome of the story.

7. Read all the dialogue in your manuscript out loud. Notice the places you wince, or change the words on the page to sound better to the ear. Revise those passages.

ELEVEN

Next Steps

You did it. You finished your revisions. You improved every aspect of your novel, from characters to setting to plot. You've touched every scene, every paragraph, and every sentence. You're intimately familiar with your novel, and you've got strong emotions about it. You either think your book is brilliant or you never want to see it again. It's totally normal to bounce between those two emotions. Every writer gets up in his feelings at this point.

That intimate familiarity and strong emotion is just another way of saying that you've lost your objectivity. It's impossible for a writer to truly know how his story will be received until he gets a reader's critique.

Once you've taken your novel as far as you can on your own, it's time to share it with others. Read through the entire manuscript one more time, preferably out loud, and then recruit some beta readers.

Beta Readers

Beta readers are generous souls who agree to read your novel and tell you what they think of it. This is a volunteer job, not a paid service. Writers exchange manuscripts, either one-to-one or on a rotating basis.

Finding good betas can be a challenge, but every writer is desperate for feedback, so the more beta reads you *give*, the more you'll *get*. Start with your own circle of writer friends. If you don't have writer friends, make some. Immediately.

Offer to read for your writing buddies, even if they write in a different genre from you. Do the best job you can for them. Give them sincere, honest, helpful feedback on their manuscripts. Giving a critique helps you as much as getting one. Every critique you give hones your editing skills. It's also good karma. When you have a manuscript in need of feedback, your friends will step up.

Try to get more than one beta read on each manuscript. You need more than one person's opinion to get a consensus. It's always instructive to see where betas agree and where they differ.

A beta reader will give you a reader's perspective. Do they like the protagonist? Do they understand your plot? They'll tell you what's confusing. They'll point out inconsistencies and plot holes. A good beta reader will also tell you what you're doing right. You need to know this. It's not about your ego. It's about knowing what's working so you can do more of it.

Don't expect your betas to do copyedits for you. That's not their job. Typos will sneak in, but you should make sure your manuscript is as clean as possible before asking for a read. Betas are great at pointing out areas that need revising, but they can't do those fixes for you. They also can't tell you what genre your book is, or how to make it more marketable.

Beta reads always take longer than you want them to. Reading takes time. Reading critically takes even more time. Tragically, your book is not your beta's number one priority. She's squeezing your book into her already full life. You're going to have to wear your patient pants for several weeks, possibly a month.

When you get your manuscript back, thank your beta fully and sincerely, no matter how long it took or how much of the critique you agree with. Your beta has done you a huge favor, and gratitude is in order.

You have to accept feedback in whatever form the beta gives you. Some betas write in the margins. Some write comments in a separate document. Some do both. Some write terse comments and some practically write an entire novel back to you. Betas are going to do what betas are going to do.

When you receive your critique, your first job is to thank your beta. The second is to read through the comments. The third is to put the manuscript away for twenty-four hours, while you have a pity party in private.

It's going to sting. No matter how eager you were

for this feedback, no matter how many times you've been through this process, it's still going to hurt. The beta reader's assignment was to find everything wrong with your book, so fulfilling the assignment means telling you exactly what's not working. It's a lot to take in. Let your emotions cool for a day, and I promise that the feedback will seem different tomorrow. It will probably be exactly what you needed to hear.

If something isn't clear, you can ask your beta questions, but don't put her on the spot, making her justify her critique. You will never agree one hundred percent with anyone's feedback, and you can keep or discard any of your beta reader's suggestions, with no hard feelings. Always value relationships over critiques. A single beta read isn't worth losing a friendship over.

Freelance Editors

When you hear the word *editor*, you probably think of someone who works for a big publishing house, but a freelance editor works directly for the author. This is the kind of editor you hire when you're going to self-publish your work. The subtitle of this book is *How to Be Your Own Editor*, but you should also consider having a professional look at your work before you publish.

A freelance editor's only job is to make your book better. She's helping you make your book the best version of itself that it can possibly be. Your editor is bringing your book to its full potential, meaning that she's helping you communicate exactly what you meant to communicate. To a freelance editor, the book itself is the most important thing.

A freelance editor answers only to you. She doesn't have a boss or a sales team changing your book for the marketplace. A freelance editor also works on *your* timeline. Big publishers are glacially slow, but when you hire your own editor, she's going to work on your book right away, and have it back to you in a few weeks.

Freelance editors aren't hard to find. They're everywhere. There are cheap ones who will simply run your book through grammar-checking software. There are expensive ones who used to work for Random House or Simon and Schuster and expect that same paycheck as freelancers. There are editors at every price point and ability in between.

A quality edit is labor-intensive, and it's not something that a computer can do. You're paying for an editor's time and experience. You need to make sure you get full value for those dollars, so be sure your editor is a good fit. Not every editor is right for every book. You've got to get recommendations and you've got to shop around. Always ask for a sample edit. Any honest editor will edit a sample for free. I edit the first thirty pages for my samples. Some editors I know do ten. A sample edit is an ideal way to see if your style and the editor's style are a match.

Use your beta readers first, and revise your manuscript on your own before you start paying professionals. An editor will give better suggestions on a manuscript that's already fairly polished. She won't waste time fixing beginner problems and can concentrate on higher-level improvements.

Know what kind of edits you're buying. There are three kinds of editing. Developmental editing includes big-picture stuff like plot, characterization, pacing, and theme. It's a story-focused edit. Copyedits cover grammar, spelling, word choice, and consistency. It's a language-focused edit. Proofreading is all about fixing typos. Be clear on what kind of edits you're buying before you hand over your hard-earned money.

Publishers

Approaching publishers can be a daunting process. Not only are you sending your novel to strangers, but those strangers are the gatekeepers to your dream. There's a lot at stake for you as a writer at this stage of the process. It can be easy to talk yourself out of even trying. The fear associated with sharing your novel with publishers comes from the unknown. The trick is to educate yourself, so you won't get taken in by shady actors.

The internet is filled with resources. It's also filled

with scammers. Research. (The website *Writer Beware* is a great place to start.) Ask your writer friends for a reality check. Hold tight to your wallet. When you're dealing with traditional publishing, the money always flows toward the writer. If anyone asks you to pay, run.

Learn about legitimate publishers and agents, looking for those who publish or represent books like yours. Write the best query letter you can. Approach them with professionalism. Don't expect any feedback at this stage. Form letters and unanswered emails are the norm.

If you secure the services of an agent, their job is to sell your novel. Some agents will ask you to do a revision for them, focused on marketability. Agents, through their experience in publishing, think they know what readers want. If you trust your agent and the revisions align with your vision for the novel, go ahead and do them. Or you might prefer an agent who wants to sell your novel as-is. In either case, it's better not to romanticize the agent-author relationship. This is a business arrangement.

When dealing with the big New York publishers, an agent makes the sale, and then you'll work with an in-house editor, who will edit your book. The editor is like a beta reader with authority. She's not making suggestions. She's making mandates. It comes from a good place. Your editor wants to shape your novel to give it a better chance in the market, so it will sell more copies. You don't have to make all the requested changes, but if you protest, you'd better have a good reason for doing so. Traditional publishers also provide copyedits and proofreading. These are done by assistants or hired out to freelancers.

A similar process happens at small presses. However, you're likely to get more hands-on editing there. Small press editors are passionate about the books they acquire and since they publish fewer of them, they can give each one more attention—that is, if they have the time. Small press editors tend to be just as overworked as their big-publisher colleagues.

How to be Done

You're done with your novel when your novel is the best you can make it. Way back when you first started writing this novel, you had a vision for it. You saw the story unfold in your imagination. When you're done, the story on the page matches that vision. It's compelling. It's interesting. The plot works. The characters are appealing. The scenes are in a logical order. The story evokes the emotions you intended to evoke. It's the most entertaining book you could write at this moment.

Let your work rest for a day or two, to let your feelings cool. Write a query or some jacket copy. Write a logline or an elevator pitch if you're so inclined. Start looking for agents or start looking for a freelance editor.

And then *move on*. Don't keep circling back, fiddling endlessly, trying to make your one, singular book into the perfect novel. Perfect doesn't exist. All you can do is write the best novel that *you* can write. When you've achieved that? That's when your book is done.

A Second Look

1. Let your manuscript rest for a week.

2. If you have friends who write, offer to beta read for them, and ask if they'd beta read for you. If you don't have friends who write, network in the local writer community, and keep at it until you have a good number of steady beta partnerships.

3. If you're going to self-publish your novel, research freelance editors to find one that's a good fit for you.

4. If you're going to seek traditional publishing, research agents. Research publishers and small presses, but be mindful of vanity presses and other scams. Use watchdogs like writerbeware.com to assist you in being a discerning author.

5. When your book is as good as you can make it, move on to the next project as soon as possible.

TWELVE

You Got This!

Now is your chance.

Your second draft is your opportunity to make your novel everything you want it to be, even if "second draft" means several passes through the manuscript. Your imagination and your perseverance will combine with your love for your story to create something extraordinary.

There will be hard days. It will look like chaos at times. You'll have moments of fear and doubt. But there will also be moments of total clarity. Scenes will slot themselves into the right place. Description will become vivid. Characters will come to life. Dialogue will sharpen to a point. You'll start to understand your novel on a deeper level, as the layers gracefully connect. Every moment you spend rethinking, rearranging, and redrafting will be worth it.

Especially if you don't give up.

The benefits of editing your own novel go way beyond fixing your current manuscript. You're not only making yourself a better editor, you're making yourself a better *writer*.

Editing your own novel teaches you valuable skills. You're learning what works, what doesn't, and why. Once you have those tools in your writerly toolbox, they're yours for life. You'll use those techniques the next time you revise a novel, but you'll also use them proactively when writing your next book.

You should have goals while you're editing, but only focus on goals you can control. Your edits can't make agents take your book, or make buyers buy it. You're not editing to make your book marketable, or to guarantee good reviews. Things you *can* control include revising the big turning point scenes, or making sure all the description is in the hero's voice, or making sure the stakes intensify at the right moment. You can control the pace of your editing, deciding how many hours per week you'll dedicate to working on your book, and sticking to it. You can exchange beta reads with another author. You can finish your second draft.

Things you can't control make you freeze up. They make you doubt. They remove your agency and make you feel powerless. However, if you only focus on what you can control, you've got action steps. Once you take that first action, you can take another, and another, until your book is the best version of itself.

Don't forget to reward yourself along the way. Sometimes the editing itself is the reward, as you grow your confidence and see your book getting better and better, but external rewards are just as important. Rewards don't have to be big, expensive, or full of calories. My favorite reward is to turn on music I love and have a dance party for one. Try it. You'll be amazed at how good it feels. If you do this after every editing session, your brain will soon associate editing with celebration and fun.

Never edit to the point where you lose your love for your novel. You're not trying to reform your book into perfection. You're trying to make it optimally entertaining. At the end of the day, revision isn't meant to make your book flawless. It's meant to make it enjoyable. Certain scenes, in a certain order, please readers and give them the emotional experience they want. Clear writing makes those scenes effortless to read. When the author is definitive and specific, with a strong voice, the reader falls into the story, bringing her imagination along for the ride. That's what good editing can do for your novel.

If you've done what you set out to do, revising your novel to your satisfaction, then you can confidently send it into the world, knowing that no matter what happens next, you can hold your head up proudly. If you've edited your novel to this standard, then no rejection can hurt you, and no bad reviews can touch you, because *you* know that your novel is the best you can make it. Don't publish it or send it to agents until it reaches that standard, but once it does, send it into the world with pride.

Your Free Book
_____

Feeling overwhelmed with your revision? You're not alone!

Revision **Mindset**

How to Start Your Revision and
Stick to it Until the Final Word

Alex Kourvo
author of *The Big-Picture Revision Checklist*

Revision is where good stories become great. It's also a lot of work. But with the right mindset, it can be one of the most rewarding parts of the writing process.

Revision Mindset will help you approach your novel's revision with clarity, confidence, and even joy.

You'll learn how to see your novel with fresh eyes, how to stay open to discovery, and how to set up a realistic schedule that fits your life. You'll also find advice on managing self-doubt, asking for support from loved ones, and how to know when you're done.

You'll come away with practical strategies and a renewed sense of motivation, ready to transform your draft into the best version of your story.

Download your free copy of *Revision Mindset* today by visiting AlexKourvo.com/FreeBook

Acknowledgements

Thank you to Christine, Clif, Kirsten, Michael, and Sara for valuable advice.

And especially to Bethany. I couldn't have written this book without you.

A huge thank you to the Ann Arbor District Library, and the attendees of the Emerging Writers Workshop. I can't wait to see all your books on the shelves.

About the Author

Alex Kourvo loves books. She reads them, writes them, edits them, reviews them, and teaches other people how to write them. Sometimes, she dreams about books.

Alex is an editor for small presses and private clients. She's also the co-founder of the Emerging Writers Workshop at the Ann Arbor District Library, where she's given monthly writing classes since 2014.

Alex lives in Michigan, in the perfect town, on the perfect street, in the perfect house. She loves key lime pie, puppies, sunbeams, and new books to read.

You can find out more about Alex's editing services at her website.

AlexKourvo.com